Oxford Reading Tree

Teacher's Guide 5

Robins and Jackdaws Stages 6–11

Compiled by James Driver, Roderick Hunt, and Tish Keech

Oxford University Press

Oxford University Press, Great Clarendon Street, Oxford OX2 6DP

Oxford   New York
Athens   Auckland   Bangkok   Bogota   Buenos Aires   Calcutta   Cape Town   Chennai
Dar es Salaam   Delhi   Florence   Hong Kong   Istanbul   Karachi   Kuala Lumpur
Madrid   Melbourne   Mexico City   Mumbai   Nairobi   Paris   São Paolo   Singapore
Taipei   Tokyo   Toronto   Warsaw

and associated companies in
Berlin   Ibadan

Oxford is a trade mark of Oxford University Press

First published 1996
Reprinted 1997, 1998

ISBN 0 19 916498 3

The Authors and Publisher would like to thank the many advisers who have helped with
the development of the Oxford Reading Tree and the original Teacher's Guides. We
should particularly like to mention:
Roy Ilsley, Tricia Kirkham, Oliver Gregory, Joy Kinnings,

For help with this new edition Teacher's Guide 5 we should particularly like to mention:
Jane Barker, Di Evans, Chris Lewis, Edna McBride, Gaynor Stubbs.

Edited by Elizabeth Paren of Paren and Stacey Editorial Consultants.
Designed by Design Section, Frome.
Printed in Great Britain.

Illustrations by Jan Brychta, cover illustration by John Eastwood

Contents

Teacher's Guide 5

Oxford Reading Tree Stages	Stories and Plays	Treetops	Language Resources and Branch Library

14

13 — Treetops Teacher's Guide 1

12

11 — Teacher's Guide 5 — Robins and Jackdaws

Robins and More Robins
20 stories for more competent readers who can progress quickly. Sentence structure and language are more demanding than Owls and Magpies at these stages.

Oxford Reading Tree Treetops
A new series of structured fiction for 7–11 year olds which may be introduced at Stage 10 and continuing up to Stage 14.

Magpies
12 stories which develop in complexity for the average child.

10 — Teacher's Guide 4 — Woodpeckers

Jackdaws Reading and Spelling Tests

9 — Teacher's Guide 4 — Woodpeckers

Jackdaws Anthologies and More Jackdaws Anthologies
20 anthologies of stories and factual information around a theme aimed at the more mature reader

8 — Teacher's Guide 3 — Owls and Magpies

7

Woodpeckers
10 anthologies of stories and poems to reinforce work on phonics. (Phonic Workbooks may be introduced from Stage 3 onwards.)

Owls Storybooks
22 magic key stories for the average child.

Owls Playscripts
6 magic key playscripts adapted from the Owls Storybooks.

Owls Board Games

6

5 — Teacher's Guide 2 — Stages 4-5

Stage 5 Playscripts

Language Master Cards

4

Stage 3 More Wrens

Sparrows and More Sparrows
16 books of extra reading practice for children who need more at Stages 3 and 4.

Extended Stories Photocopy Masters

Context Cards

3 — Stages 2 and 3 Wrens
Patterned storybooks offer extra reading practice for children who need further consolidation of high frequency vocabulary.

2

Sequencing Cards Photocopy Masters

Trunk
66 books which form the core of the scheme. All children progress up the trunk to the top of Stage 5.

1 — Teacher's Guide 1 — Stages 1-3

Teacher's Guide 5
Robins and Jackdaws

Woodpeckers — bird illustration

Flopover Book
The essential starting point of the Reading Tree.

Word Cards

12 picture books to reinforce storying and pre-reading skills.

Robins and Jackdaws

Key to symbols

Software/Audio	Poetry	Rhyme and Analogy	Fact Finders	Oxford Reading Tree Stages
				14
				13
				12
				11
	Jackdaws Poetry and More Jackdaws Poetry			10
	20 books which reflect the themes in the Jackdaws Anthologies. For competent readers with a mature interest level.		Unit F Our environment	9
			Teacher's Guide 2 Units D-F	8
	Conkers Poetry and More Conkers Poetry		Unit E Where people live	7
			Unit D Food	6
	Catkins Poetry and More Catkins Poetry	Story Rhyme Photocopy Masters / Rhyme and Analogy Teacher's Guide		5
Stage 4 More Storytapes accompany Stage 4 More Sparrows and Stage 4 More Stories Pack A		Story Rhyme Tapes	Unit C Houses and homes	4
Storytapes accompany stories at Stages 2, 3, 4, and Sparrows / More Storytapes accompany Stage 2 & 3 More Stories Packs A & B / Stage 3 Talking Stories / Stage 3 More Talking Stories A	Acorns Poetry and More Acorns Poetry	Story Rhymes Shared reading from Stage 1. Independent reading from Stage 5.	Unit B Families / Teacher's Guide 1 Units A-C	3
Stage 2 Stories / Stage 2 Wrens Storytapes / Stage 2 Talking Stories		Alphabet Photocopy Masters / Card Games	Unit A Myself	2
First Storytapes accompany Stage 1 Picture Storybooks / Talking Stories Stage 2 More Talking Stories A / Wrens Stage 2 Talking Stories		Tabletop Alphabet Pack / Alphabet Frieze		1

Key to symbols

- Flopover Book
- Individual storybook/playscript/pupils' book
- Extended Stories
- Big Books
- Teacher's Guide
- Storytapes
- Talking Stories/Floppy disk
- Talking Stories/CD ROM
- Videos
- Workbooks
- BL Branch Library
- P Photocopy Masters
- SR Story Rhyme pupils' book

Books and materials illustrated in half-strength colour are not covered in this Teacher's Guide.

Stages 1–5	chronological age 5–6
Stages 6–9 Owls/Magpies	chronological age 6–7
Robins and Jackdaws are suitable for competent and mature readers	chronological age 6–9
Stages 10–14 Treetops	chronological age 7–11

For further information phone the **Oxford Reading Tree Care-line**

(01865) 267881.

Introduction

Schools throughout the country are continuing to help with the programme and are trialling new materials with great success. The *Oxford Reading Tree* is still growing and the publishers would welcome comments and suggestions from you if you would like to be involved in its development.

If you want to participate in the development of *Oxford Reading Tree,* write to OXED, Oxford University Press, Walton Street, Oxford OX2 6DP. There is also a Care-line for *Oxford Reading Tree* users who want help or advice: 01865 267881.

This new *Teacher's Guide 5* covers the *Robins* and *Jackdaws* branches at Stages 6 to 11 of the *Oxford Reading Tree.* The guide maintains and extends the philosophy and approach of the earlier editions of this guide and of the earlier stages of the *Oxford Reading Tree.* It also provides suggestions and photocopiable materials to reinforce children's understanding of the text and to extend their reading skills.

The *Oxford Reading Tree* has grown with the encouragement and advice of practising teachers both in mainstream primary and infant schools and in special needs support teams and special schools, where the materials have been found to be effective and popular.

Many suggestions have been received from teachers who are experienced users of the programme, and they have been incorporated into the revised guide.

The *Oxford Reading Tree* has also benefited from the feedback that has been received from its wide use in schools as far afield as South Africa and New Zealand, the United States, Pakistan, and many English-speaking schools throughout Europe.

How to use this guide

Teacher's Guide 5 has a 'General introduction to the whole programme' on pages 12–13 which gives an overview of the *Oxford Reading Tree* approach, similar to *Teacher's Guides 1* and *2*, but with specific reference to the *Robins* and *Jackdaws* materials at Stages 6-11.

It is recommended that you look first at the 'What is in this guide?' chart on pages 10–11, then have a general look through the guide to familiarize yourself with the range of its contents. You will find it useful to read all the introductory sections (pages 14–32).

What is in this guide?

General introduction to the whole programme

(pages 12–13)

Describes the *Oxford Reading Tree* approach to the teaching of reading

Using the Oxford Reading Tree

(pages 14–16)

Explains:

♦ the structure of the programme ♦ the materials for *Robins* and *Jackdaws* ♦ how the materials are to be used

Putting the Oxford Reading Tree approach into practice

(pages 17–22)

Explains:

♦ how to make questioning effective ♦ the five-step approach to *Robins* and *Jackdaws*

♦ how to work with groups ♦ the ways in which wider reading skills can be developed

Questions you may want to ask	(pages 23–24)
Assessment	(pages 25–30)
Parental involvement	(pages 31–32)

Robins and More Robins

INTRODUCTION (pages 34–36)

Includes:

♦ the aims of the *Robins* branch
♦ what the materials are
♦ how to use the materials

Jackdaws and More Jackdaws

INTRODUCTION (pages 138–143)

Includes:

♦ the aims of the *Jackdaws* branch
♦ what the materials are
♦ how to use the materials

Discussion pointers and general discussion

Language activities

Further activities

Assessment

General introduction to the whole programme

The approach

The *Oxford Reading Tree* is a flexible reading programme for primary children (with further extension reading provided by *Treetops*, see page 13). It addresses the reading needs and development of the whole child by building primarily on the importance of story in the learning experience of all children. At the same time it recognizes the wide range of skills that the child needs to acquire in learning to read.

By the time children reach the *Robins* and *Jackdaws* they begin to rely less and less on a range of cues and clues, such as illustration, regular and ordered syntax and the page-by-page discussion. By this stage the children have built a considerable sight vocabulary, so they are able to recognize words easily and quickly when reading. This rapid recognition of words enables them to predict unknown words. In this way they create the context that allows them to 'fill the gaps' when they come to unfamiliar words or phrases. By reading often, and through shared reading, children gain rapidly in confidence and move quickly towards independence.

The importance of talk and context
The *Oxford Reading Tree* is rooted in talk. As the children grow in confidence, it is easy to place less emphasis on discussion around each storybook. However, there are still important advantages in encouraging the children to talk about the story before they read it and it takes only a few minutes.

Each child's response consists of her understanding and interpretation of what the author and illustrator are trying to say. It has to do with the making of meaning and the identification of experience. By talking about a story, and listening to others talk about it, children are learning to become both creative and critical readers.

Group discussions about a story can be very effective because children learn from each other, discovering insights and making observations that they are able to share. To help you when discussing the story with a group of children, discussion questions are provided for many of the stories and there are general discussion questions to stimulate talk around the themes of the stories.

Language and further activities
Children's learning can be supported by using the range of language activities and further activities suggested in this guide.

Three photocopiable language activities are included in this guide for each of the *Robins* storybooks. In most cases these consist of a comprehension activity sheet, a creative writing activity sheet and a third sheet dealing with grammar, instructional writing, cloze procedure or sequencing.

There are also three activity sheets for each *Jackdaws* anthology. These provide a range of lively and informal activities concentrating on the core skills of comprehension, grammar and punctuation.

The activities cover many aspects of the National Curriculum in England and Wales and the Scottish Office Guidelines, English Language 5–14. For grids showing specific skills/activities provided by the language activities please see page 64 for the *Robins* and *More Robins* and page 155 for the *Jackdaws* and *More Jackdaws*.

The further activities for the *Robins* and *Jackdaws* provide in total six ideas for planning cross-curricular work, incorporating the settings and themes of many of the storybooks and anthologies. They are not intended to cover all aspects of the National Curriculum but are suggestions for developing some storybook themes where these fit into your programme.

For more detailed information, see pages 125 and 216.

Further materials

Within the *Oxford Reading Tree* are also:
- a range of poetry linked to the themes and stages of the stories
- a programme of information books called *Fact Finders* which are grouped around popular infant topics
- materials that introduce phonological awareness through rhyme and analogy.

There is also a range of stories called *Treetops* for children who are reaching independence in their reading. This series comprises a range of fiction which has been written in a variety of styles to accommodate the differing strengths and interests of children from the age of seven to eleven.

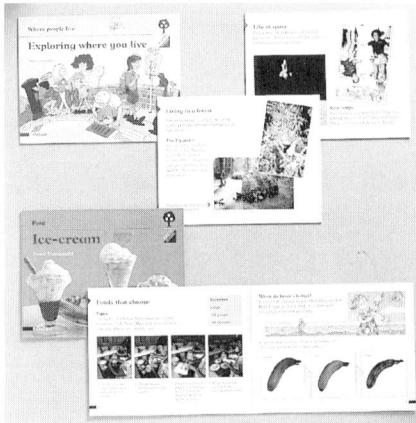

Using the Oxford Reading Tree

The *Oxford Reading Tree* is divided into eleven levels or stages with three further stages provided by *Treetops*. Stage 1 teaches children important pre-reading skills; Stages 2–5 introduce specific reading skills which are developed as children progress through Stages 6–11.

Why a tree?

The 'tree' is not only a diagram representing the way that the *Oxford Reading Tree* is structured, it is also an analogy for the way the programme develops reading.

With its roots, main trunk and branches, the *Oxford Reading Tree* aims to provide a programme that can be used flexibly, accommodating both the variable rates of reading growth in an individual child, and the differences that are bound to exist in both the development and attainment of all children.

These differences are thrown into their sharpest focus once children are in their second year in school. The *Robins* and *Jackdaws* branches are designed to accommodate these differences. A few children will be looking for more challenging and demanding books. Some will be moving quickly towards independent reading, but will still need support and encouragement. Many will still need texts that are familiar in style and format.

The Robins and Jackdaws

Robins and More Robins
Stages 6–10

Robins and *Jackdaws* form two separate branches of the *Oxford Reading Tree*. It is recommended that all children complete the trunk storybooks as far as *Magpies* Stage 9. Children who need the accelerated reading progress offered by the *Robins* can then be introduced to *Robins* Stage 6 and work their way through to *Robins* Stage 10. Children who are ready to enjoy the challenge of a greater variety of reading may read the *Jackdaws* anthologies alongside *Robins,* or after completing *Robins.*

The Robins storybooks
Robins cover Stages 6–10, and have been written for competent readers who are beginning to progress quickly and need slightly wider and more demanding reading, but who still need the security of familiar reading book formats.

The *Robins* broaden the children's reading with stories written and illustrated by a variety of authors and illustrators. The familiar characters of Biff, Chip, Kipper and friends still feature in some of the storybooks, with new characters, such as William and Hamid, and Kate and Jo, appearing in others.

The *Robins* storybooks make greater demands than the *Owls* and *Magpies* storybooks on the reader, incorporating a variety of settings both rural and urban. Many of the stories focus on situations and events which lend themselves to discussion and reflection. The relationship between text and illustration is less tightly controlled, and the sentence structure, while remaining straightforward and uncluttered, is less restricted thus allowing each *Robins* story to be written in an appropriate style.

The Jackdaws anthologies

The *Jackdaws* are written for competent independent readers with a mature interest level who need enjoyable reading material that will challenge and develop their reading skills further. They are anthologies which cover Stages 8–11 and offer three different types of writing – an adventure, traditional tales and factual material linked to themes. The branch is thus designed to provide writing of different genres, stimulating the independent reader with a variety of styles. The illustrations also offer variety, the elements being illustrated in different styles.

While there are poetry anthologies available throughout the *Oxford Reading Tree*, the *Jackdaws* poetry anthologies relate specifically to the themes of the *Jackdaws* story anthologies.

How do Robins and Jackdaws differ?

There is some overlap between the stages covered by *Robins* (Stages 6–10) and *Jackdaws* (Stages 8–11), but the demands on the reader differ. *Robins* storybooks have one story which usually has a linear chronology. *Jackdaws* include two different story genres as well as factual information, all based on a common theme. In the *Jackdaws*, sentence structure and vocabulary are much freer than in the *Robins*, and there is more text on each page. *Jackdaws* raise ideas and issues which are appropriate for children with a more mature interest level.

Using Robins and Jackdaws

The aim of the *Robins* and *Jackdaws* branches of the *Oxford Reading Tree* is to provide a choice of enjoyable reading material and to encourage children to become effective readers, rather than decoders of words on a page.

At this stage of their reading development, when children are reading independently, it is easy to assume that they are emerging as real readers, bringing their own knowledge to bear on what they read, and under-standing and absorbing the ideas and concepts contained in a story. This is not always the case. Not all children who learn to decode, learn to become effective readers.

Reading is, after all, an acquired skill of a high order. It involves comprehension, interpretation and perception; it requires a knowledge of words and an understanding of their shifts of meaning in different contexts or in relation to other words; it demands the reader's involvement with the story and calls on her ability to visualize a situation described only in words; it invites the readers to put themselves in the place of the characters in the

---

Jackdaws and More Jackdaws
Stages 8–11

Robins
- linear chronology
- varied settings
- different styles
- straightforward sentence structure
- some familiar characters

Jackdaws
- anthologies linked by common theme
- two different story genres
- some non-fiction writing
- freer sentence structure and vocabulary
- issues appropriate for mature interest level

story and, vicariously, to think their thoughts, experience their sensations and appreciate their emotions.

Talking and thinking about stories and listening to what others think and say about them is central to the philosophy of the *Oxford Reading Tree*. At this stage of their reading development it is important that the children are allowed some autonomy in their discussions about the stories, working in groups and talking and listening to each other's views.

In each section of this guide, questions are provided to encourage children to talk about the characters, the plot, the storyline, incidents, feelings and emotions. They help children to understand the reasons that lie behind what happens in any story and they give a sense of time and location.

We would, of course, always recommend that you are familiar with the books before giving them to the children. This is necessary for you to assess their suitability for each individual in terms of content and level of difficulty.

The discussion pointers and general discussion

An essential step towards becoming a competent reader is the ability to understand a story, to be able to express an opinion, and to frame some questions and thoughts about it.

Suggestions for questions and discussion pointers are given in this guide. There are questions relating to each page of the *Robins* stories, as well as general questions about the story and points that arise from it. There are also general discussion questions for each *More Robins* storybook.

For the *Jackdaws* and *More Jackdaws* there are questions to introduce children to the theme of each anthology and the ideas raised in the stories. These should be discussed before children read the stories for themselves. Further questions open up discussion, encouraging children to form their own views and talk about the way each story is written.

Language activities

For each of the *Robins*, *More Robins*, *Jackdaws* and *More Jackdaws* there are three photocopiable language activity sheets. They are provided as suggestions for you to choose from and adapt to suit the needs and attainments of your particular children. For more information on the *Robins* see page 35 and on the *Jackdaws* see page 139.

Language support materials

There are five workbooks to accompany the *Robins* storybooks (see page 35). There are also two *Jackdaws Reading and Spelling Tests* which are designed to practise and assess silent reading and spelling skills (see page 140).

Putting the Oxford Reading Tree approach into practice

**The five-step approach
to *Robins* and *Jackdaws***

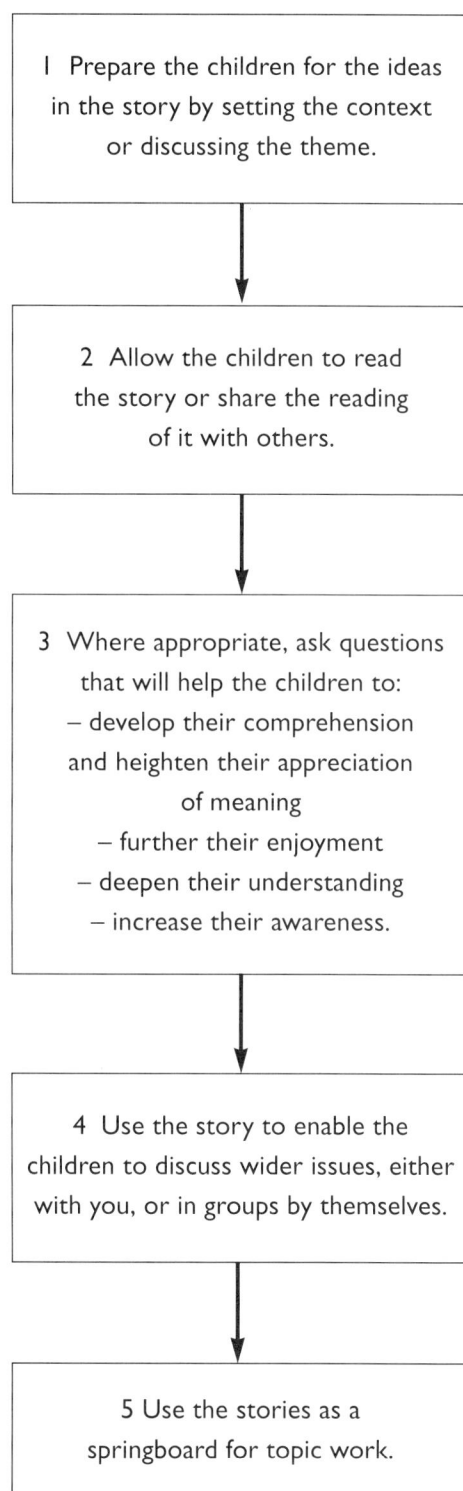

1 Prepare the children for the ideas in the story by setting the context or discussing the theme.

2 Allow the children to read the story or share the reading of it with others.

3 Where appropriate, ask questions that will help the children to:
– develop their comprehension and heighten their appreciation of meaning
– further their enjoyment
– deepen their understanding
– increase their awareness.

4 Use the story to enable the children to discuss wider issues, either with you, or in groups by themselves.

5 Use the stories as a springboard for topic work.

Effective questioning

The range of questions for each of the *Robins* and *Jackdaws* storybooks is intended to help children think about what they are seeing and hearing and to stimulate talk. These questions are simply suggestions and you can, of course, adapt or add to them as appropriate. Hopefully, children will begin to develop the ability to think of questions to ask for themselves, and this will increasingly be the case if they become used to regular discussions in small groups. (See the section on working in groups on page 18.)

In this guide, suggestions for questions and discussion pointers are given as follows:

Robins

There are questions relating to each page or double-page of the stories and general questions about the story and points that arise from it. For *More Robins* there are general discussion questions only.

Jackdaws

There are questions for each anthology which introduce the children to its theme and the ideas raised in the stories. These should be discussed before the children read the stories for themselves. Further questions open up the discussion on each story, encouraging children to form their own views and to talk about the way each story is written.

The five-step approach to Robins and Jackdaws

The diagram to the left recommends a procedure for reading a new story-book and asking questions about it. Each step should be seen as an integral part of a single approach in encouraging children to deepen their understanding and further their enjoyment of reading.

Before the story

The *Robins* and the *Jackdaws* stories benefit from a discussion which sets the context or thinks about the theme of the story. For example, in *The secret plans* (*Robins* Stage 10) many children will have a greater appreciation of the story if they understand what plans are, and what is meant by plans having to be kept secret at government level. Therefore, some preliminary discussion or explanation will enable the children to read with more understanding and depth.

During the story

If you are sharing the story with the children, suitable questions at appropriate moments are helpful in fostering understanding. It is important to be flexible when asking questions or starting discussion. You would not want to ask questions about every page of a book but it is a good idea to interject with an appropriate question when you feel the moment allows. Sometimes a pause in the reading to talk about something that has happened in the narrative will help to heighten enjoyment or understanding. It may, similarly, help to 'pick up' a flagging reader and provide momentum to the story. You may occasionally want to go back over certain pages once the children have finished the book.

After the story

Often the story will lead to valuable discussion about the points raised by the story. In *The Dump*, (*Robins* Stage 6) for example, there are a number of issues which could give rise to discussion, including a campaign to save a playground, the characters witnessing a theft, and the problem of children having suitable places to play. The children themselves may have very strong ideas about safe and satisfying places to play both in urban and in rural areas and may enjoy exploring the issues raised in the story. When a book fires the children into keen, even passionate discussion, then the reading process is working as it should.

Questions for general discussion

The discussion questions are intended to supplement your own ideas and to remind you of the potential that every aspect of a story offers for discussion and reflection.

Many in the group will have experiences they want to talk about. Discussions of this kind offer children a chance to vocalize their feelings and experiences, sometimes to come to terms with painful or difficult situations, and to feel that their opinions are valued. In this way, talking or discussing becomes a means of discovery for the child and forms a vital pre-writing experience. In addition, new topics are discussed, giving the children opportunities to broaden their vocabulary and extend their general knowledge.

Working with groups

By this stage of the programme children should be quite used to working in small groups by themselves.

The discussion questions suggested in this guide are very suitable for small group discussions. They are about the wider aspects of each story, or topics relating to it. You will want to be selective, adapting them to suit the children's ability and interests.

When organizing small, self-motivated groups you may find it useful and more productive to suggest the children work to a particular goal, giving them a time limit before asking them to report back or share what they have done. Some discussion groups may work better if the children draw up a simple agenda, or work through a small list of points or questions.

Group activities work well if the children are given the opportunity to share what they have done with others. This can be done simply by your sitting in with the group encouraging and valuing what they are doing, but it is most effective if groups come together and listen to each other's conclusions. The groups will work best of all if they know they are working towards a simple presentation or summary, with the other groups as an audience.

Modes of thinking

The five modes of thinking

Reporting

Projecting

Reasoning

Deciding

Predicting

When the children are discussing a storybook, bear in mind the ways in which they can think about the story. Five of these ways are:

Reporting

This involves: recalling events in the story, recounting the sequence of events, retelling the story.

Projecting

This involves: empathizing with a character; projecting into his or her thoughts and feelings.

Reasoning

This involves: thinking about why things happen in the way they do; asking what might have happened instead; understanding how one event influenced another.

Deciding

This mode is concerned with making a choice independent of or complementary to something in the story.

Predicting

This involves predicting what is going to happen next.

Developing strategies

Important associated skills

Talking

Asking questions

Thinking

Listening

A child's ability to read in the widest sense is enhanced by the development of the associated skills of talking, thinking, questioning and listening.

Children can develop both thinking and listening skills by asking questions. They can be encouraged to find ways of arriving at the maximum amount of information from a single question; of getting to a solution through elimination, of grouping, creating sets, and listing ideas that form, say, similarities, opposites, families, constituents, and so on.

The following suggestions incorporate ideas for developing skills in these areas:

Making lists

Getting children to list things, working in pairs or groups, helps them to pool their ideas.

Talking points

Encourage children to ask open-ended questions based on the storybooks for which there are any number of answers, all of which are right. For example, using *The Dump* (*Robins* Stage 6) questions might be 'Why were Lenny and his friends "fed up"'? (page 13) or 'Why was Lenny excited?' (pages 16/17).

You and the children may like to collect pictures from newspapers and magazines that make good conversation pieces, and pose such questions as: 'What's going to happen next?'; 'What caused that?' or 'What would you say to that?'. This could extend into a writing activity.

Creating connections

You could collect interesting pictures. Spread them out on the floor and ask each child to choose any two and create or invent a connection between them. For example, a picture of a lorry full of fish and a footballer might produce the connection: 'This footballer is really fit because he eats fish every night'. The aim of the game is for children to be as imaginative as possible. Look for opportunities to extend this activity into group or individual writing work.

Predicting from incomplete information

The idea here is for the children to make predictions or draw conclusions from incomplete or partial information. Choose a picture that would make a good talking point, but show children only a part of it by sliding it, bit by bit, out of an envelope. As more of the picture is revealed, children have to modify their initial ideas. A different version of this activity is given below.

Frame game

Find a large piece of card (about one and a half times times larger than one of the reading books when opened) and cut a small window in the card approximately 5 cm x 6 cm.

Choose a picture from the storybook and select a detail – one or two figures (not the main characters), or an object associated with the main incident on the page. Slide the card over the page so that only the detail is revealed.

When playing the game children answer questions about the detail in the frame, and relate it to the picture.

The example shown to the left is of the shop assistant in the department store in the story *William and the dog* (*Robins* Stage 7) and it shows her reaction when Toffee leaps on to a counter to steal a fish.

Children may be able to think of their own questions for each frame, or you may like to ask particular questions, pitching them according to the ability of the children. However, a number of general questions could be written out on a 'question master's' card, and these could be used as the basis for each picture.

- ◆ Who/What is this?
- ◆ What has just happened?
- ◆ What is happening in the rest of the picture?
- ◆ Where is it taking place?
- ◆ What's going to happen next?

You could ask the children to develop the information into a story or a poem, for example, 'What do you think the lady told her children when she got home from work that evening?' or 'Write a poem about a naughty dog'.

Asking the right questions

You could either pretend to be another person or bring someone unknown into the classroom. The person should have agreed beforehand to answer any questions the children may ask. The children then ask the person any questions they like to find out about them.

Impose a time limit on the questioning. Once this is reached, the children should pool all the information they have acquired. They can then analyze the kind of questions that produce the best response. Some questions will have produced only a yes or no answer, while others will have been open-ended enough for the person to give much more information.

The children could try questioning for a second time. This time you could score 1, 2 or 3 points for the types of questions the children ask.

Other games

The postcard game

Make a series of 'postcards' written from different locations in the stories. Read the 'postcards' aloud and ask the children to guess which book and which location within a book is being described. Children could then draw pictures to go on the fronts of the cards.

The comprehension game

For each book, make a series of cards, with or without a picture. On each card write an inferential question. Children, in turn, pick a card from the pile, read the question aloud and answer it. If the question is answered to the satisfaction of the other players, award up to 4 or 5 points, and move counters along a track. If the answer is challenged or disputed, players may refer to the book. If the challenge is incorrect, an extra two points could be awarded. The following examples come from *The emergency* (*Robins* Stage 8).

1 Were Hamid and William both reading comics in the park? (1 point)
2 Why didn't Toffee like being on the long rope? (4 points)
3 How do you know Mrs Lacey had not been lying on the floor all night? (4 points)
4 How do you know that Mrs Knight didn't have a telephone? (3 points).

The storybooks as starting points for cross-curricular work

The *Robins* and *Jackdaws* lend themselves to topic-based activities. Children may explore their themes further, giving an impetus to developing a study within other areas of the curriculum, or the storybooks and their themes can be woven into an existing topic.

The Further activities sections of this guide provide ideas for using the storybooks as starting points for topics on caring for and helping others, school, holidays and visits (*Robins*); and on tricks and disguises, buildings and transport (*Jackdaws*). They cover many curricular areas but are intended as suggestions only.

Questions you may want to ask about the Robins and Jackdaws

How do I know which children should read up the Robins or Jackdaws branches?

It is recommended that *all* children complete the Trunk storybooks as far as *Magpies* Stage 9. Children who need the accelerated reading progress offered by the *Robins* can then be introduced to *Robins* Stage 6 and work their way through to *Robins* Stage 10. Children who are ready to enjoy the challenge of a greater variety of reading may read the *Jackdaws* anthologies alongside *Robins*, or after completing *Robins*.

Who will benefit from reading Robins?

The *Robins* are slightly more complex than the *Owls* storybooks and they introduce some new characters. This branch has been devised for children who are confident readers and ready to move towards independent reading but who still need the security of some of the well-known characters in familiar storybook formats.

How do Robins develop reading skills?

This *Teacher's Guide* provides support and guidance for using *Robins* storybooks. The approach described in this guide encourages children to become 'readers', able to appreciate the development of the story, and its characters, rather than only being able to decode words. Questions to accompany the storybooks are included providing starting points for talking about incidents in the story and characters' responses. The activity sheets develop comprehension, reference and further language skills, exposing children to a variety of written formats.

Who will benefit from reading Jackdaws?

The *Jackdaws* offer three different types of writing – an adventure, traditional tales and factual material linked to themes. They are written for competent readers with a mature interest level who need enjoyable reading material that will challenge and develop their reading skills further. There is no reason why these children should not read all the *Owls* and *Magpies* (see *Teacher's Guide 3*), interspersed with *Robins* or *Jackdaws* at the appropriate level.

How do Jackdaws develop reading skills?

This *Teacher's Guide* provides support and guidance for using the *Jackdaws* anthologies. Discussion questions introduce children to the ideas and themes raised in each story, and these should be discussed before the children read the anthologies themselves. Further questions open up discussions on the story, encouraging children to form their own views and talk about the way the story is written. The *Jackdaws* activity sheets in this guide focus children's attention on the story text, develop referencing skills and provide starting points for children's own story-writing. As children read more *Jackdaws* anthologies, they will develop preferences for particular styles of writing, encouraging them to read more widely.

Is there a recommended order of reading?

Both *Robins* and *Jackdaws* move rapidly up the stages of the *Oxford Reading Tree*. A recommended order of reading is given at each Stage on the back of the storybooks, but this need not be rigidly followed.

What happens if the children are galloping through the stories?

If children read the stories too quickly you will need to ask yourself whether they are getting the most out of them. While you do not want to hold children back, the various activity and support materials suggested in this guide as well as the many ideas for writing and cross-curricular work are all important ways of ensuring that children become committed readers.

The children read these stories easily and make rapid progress, but find books outside the programme difficult.

Many children latch on to the regular and consistent sentence structure and familiar vocabulary of the *Oxford Reading Tree* storybooks and make rapid progress which they may not be able to sustain on a wider variety of books. You can ensure this does not happen by introducing them to other books outside the programme as a matter of course. This will provide a more realistic rate of progress. Children capable of acceleration through the *Oxford Reading Tree* storybooks will be those who are likely to achieve high reading attainment, so the reading of a variety of texts, both fiction and non-fiction, should form the basis of their early reading

The reading levels at Stages 8 and 9 across the Robins, Magpies and Jackdaws do not appear to be consistent. Why is this?

The language used in *Jackdaws* is more complex than *Robins*. Sentence structure and vocabulary are less tightly controlled and there is more text on each page. In the *Jackdaws* children are introduced to the language of traditional tales, to non-fiction, and to more complex narratives, so a mature response to reading is required. Many children who make rapid and easy progress up to the top of the *Oxford Reading Tree* and move onto *Jackdaws*, however, still need the security of having books that 'belong' to the programme. So, although there is some overlap across the stages, the demands of readers differ and this may appear to create some inconsistency.

There doesn't seem time to focus on all the language activities, workbooks, and further activities that are provided for each book.

The suggested activities and workbooks are all optional elements for you to tailor to individual children's needs. You will not be able to cover all the activities, nor should you attempt to.

Does it matter if I read and share a story from a higher stage, say, The holiday (Robins) or Anna's Eggs (Jackdaws) to the whole class, when some children are still at a lower stage?

Our experience has shown that children look forward to the time when they will arrive at the higher stage and will read the story for themselves. If you have a vertically grouped class younger children will find that sharing a story with older readers, and joining in a discussion about it, is an enjoyable and valuable learning experience.

Should I allow proficient readers to 're-visit' easier books?

It is a good idea to allow children to re-read a book they have enjoyed at an earlier stage. We have observed the practice in some schools of children from Year 3/Primary 4 upwards being allowed to go back into the infant classroom, to pick out and talk about books they remember with enjoyment.

One or two children have become 'hooked' on the storybooks and I can't seem to move them on to new, or more challenging, books outside the Oxford Reading Tree.

Children must be encouraged to read widely from a range of both fiction and non-fiction books, and they should make continuous progress on to books that challenge them. The *Oxford Reading Tree* should be seen as one of the stepping stones to the world of reading and it is important that children should not become stuck on, say, the 'magic key', or the William and Hamid storybooks. It may be that children who exhibit this tendency lack confidence. Try returning to your earlier techniques of sharing a new and different book on an individual basis with each child who seems to be 'stuck', and work hard on recommending and displaying a wide variety of library books in the classroom.

Assessment

To assist you in recording and assessing children's progress, the following materials are included in this guide:

◆ checklists of *Oxford Reading Tree* books within the *Robins*, *More Robins*, *Jackdaws* and *More Jackdaws*, arranged according to Stage
◆ eight passages to be used for running records at Stages 6–11
◆ a book review sheet for children to record their personal preferences.

The checklist of books

The checklist of books can be used to keep a simple quantitative record of the *Oxford Reading Tree* books the child has read at different stages and may be completed by the child himself, if you wish. This is not intended to be a complete list of all the books a child should experience whilst reading within a stage. Children should be given the opportunity to experience a wide range of books of different types from the earliest stages. Lists of other titles you may have in your class or school library related to cross-curricular topics are provided in the Further activities sections of this guide.

Running records

A running record is a method of diagnostic assessment which helps to:
◆ assess a child's fluency and accuracy
◆ identify what reading strategies a child is already using
◆ establish what help he needs to improve.

The running record is a method which allows you to analyze and record progress as part of the time you normally spend reading with children, although you may wish to arrange to do it in a quiet place at first whilst you get used to taking the record. It will also tell you if the book the child is reading is suitable for his level of reading development. The sheets provided enable you to make and keep four running records when a child is reading *Robins* and *More Robins* and four on *Jackdaws* and *More Jackdaws*.

Making a running record
The child reads a passage to you from his storybook whilst you mark the 'miscues'. (The errors are called 'miscues' because they tell us about the reading strategy which has misled the child.) You can mark the miscues and correctly read words on a copy of the passage or on a separate piece of paper. You should talk to the child about the passage, asking him to tell you what happened in it to assess his understanding. The percentage accuracy rate can then be calculated and the sort of miscues a child has made examined in detail.

You may wish to use running records to assess a child's reading at key points (for instance, when you think a child is ready to move on to the next stage) or on a regular basis. The following passages are included in this guide:

Robins and *More Robins*
Stage 6   page 132 – *The Dump* pages 20–22
Stage 7   page 133 – *The long journey* pages 16–18
Stage 9   page 134 – *Treasure hunt* pages 6–8
Stage 10   page 135 – *The holiday* pages 25–27

Jackdaws and *More Jackdaws*
Stage 8   page 223 – *Anna's eggs* pages 12–13
Stage 9   page 224 – *William and the spell* pages 8–9
Stage 10   page 225 – *Karen's adventure* page 17
Stage 11   page 226 – *The island* page 12

Each passage is approximately 100 words long so that the percentage error rate may be easily calculated. Of course, if you wish to make running records for other passages or books you can do so by simply making the record on a blank sheet of paper using the same symbols (see below) but writing in the correct text as well as the child's response when he makes an error or by placing a sheet of tracing paper over a copy of the book and marking on that.

Procedure for using a running record

I First tell the child that you are going to talk about how he is getting on with his reading and work on it together.

When you carry out a running record you should try to ensure the child is reading at the 'instructional' level, that is the level at which he is making some mistakes but understands most of what he reads. It is at this level that the child is most likely to benefit from this type of teaching and intervention.

2 Ask the child to read the passage you have chosen (or one of those provided in this book) from his storybook.

Record how he reads each word using the marks below or your own adapted version of them. It is important that the child reads without prompting as much as possible. Encourage the child to attempt unknown words but tell him a word if he asks for help or when a miscue or omission would alter the sense of the passage. Do intervene if he shows signs of becoming distressed.

Marks to use when making a reading record

correct	✔	✔ 'What do we do now?' asked William.
omission	O or circle word	O 'What do we do now?' asked William.
word told to child	T	T 'What do we do now?' asked William.
wrong response	write what the child says	said 'What do we do now?' asked William.
self-correction	write what the child says and ⒮Ⓒ	said ⒮Ⓒ 'What do we do now?' asked William.
word inserted	write what the child says and a ⋀	all 'What do we ⋀do now?' asked William. ⋀

3 Talk to the child about the passage he has just read. (Possible questions are provided for the running records passages in this guide.)
Try to talk about the passage in such a way that the questions arise naturally and to encourage expanded answers rather than just 'yes' or 'no'. Discussion of the questions should help you judge other aspects of the child's development, for example, his breadth of vocabulary, ability to report, reason and predict.

4 Calculate the percentage accuracy rate after the reading session using the method below.
Compare the accuracy rate with the notes on Levels of reading given below to ensure that the child is reading at the correct level. Analyze the types of miscue the child has made to identify the reading strategies he is already using.

On page 28 are two examples of running records, the first made on the passage itself, the second marked on a separate sheet.

Calculating the percentage accuracy rate
To score the percentage accuracy rate count the number of words read accurately (in this example 97, if self-corrections are treated as correctly read words) then calculate this as a percentage of the number of words in the passage.

For example: $\dfrac{97}{105} \times 100 = 92\%$ accuracy

Passage marked as a running record

✔ ✔ ✔ ✔ ✔ ✔ T O ✔ ✔ ✔ ✔ ✔ ✔ ✔ ✔ broken (sc) ✔
The next box was outside the cinema but when the boys got there that one was wrecked too.
✔   ✔   ✔   ✔   ✔ ✔ ✔ ✔ ✔ ✔   ✔
The windows were broken and red paint had been sprayed everywhere.
✔ ✔ ✔   said   ✔
'What a mess!' groaned Hamid.
✔ ✔ ✔ O   said   ✔
'What do we do now?' asked William.
✔   ✔ ✔ ✔ ✔ ✔ ✔ ✔ ✔ ✔ ✔ ✔ ✔ ✔ ✔
'There's another box near the park,' said Hamid, 'but it will take ages to get there.'
✔ ✔ ✔   ✔   ✔ O ✔ ✔ ✔ ✔ ✔
'Come on,' said William, 'we'll just have to run all the way.'
✔ ✔ ✔✔ T   ✔   ✔   got to ✔ ✔
They were out of breath when they reached the park.
✔ ✔ ✔ ✔ ✔ ✔   ✔   ✔
There was someone in the telephone box.
✔ ✔ ✔ ✔ ✔ ✔   ✔ ✔
'Oh no! We'll have to wait,' said Hamid.
✔   ✔   said (sc) ✔   ✔ ✔ ✔ ✔ ✔ ✔   ✔
'Don't worry,' gasped William, 'we can tell them it's an emergency.'

105 words
(97 words read accurately)

Running record marked on a separate sheet of paper

| The next box was outside the cinema but when | ✔ | ✔ | ✔ | ✔ | ✔ | ✔ | T | O | ✔ |
| the boys got there that one was wrecked too. | ✔ | ✔ | ✔ | ✔ | ✔ | ✔ | ✔ | (sc) broken | ✔ |

| The windows were broken and | ✔ | ✔ | ✔ | ✔ | ✔ |
| red paint had been sprayed everywhere. | ✔ | ✔ | ✔ | ✔ | ✔ | ✔ |

'What a mess!' groaned Hamid. ✔ ✔ ✔ said ✔

'What do we do now?' asked William. ✔ ✔ ✔ ✔ O said ✔

| 'There's another box near the park,' said Hamid, 'but | ✔ | ✔ | ✔ | ✔ | ✔ | ✔ | ✔ | ✔ | ✔ |
| it will take ages to get there.' | ✔ | ✔ | ✔ | ✔ | ✔ | ✔ | ✔ |

| 'Come on,' said William, 'we'll just | ✔ | ✔ | ✔ | ✔ | ✔ | O |
| have to run all the way.' | ✔ | ✔ | ✔ | ✔ | ✔ | ✔ |

They were out of breath when they reached the park. ✔ ✔ ✔ ✔ T ✔ ✔ got to ✔ ✔

There was someone in the telephone box. ✔ ✔ ✔ ✔ ✔ ✔ ✔

'Oh no! We'll have to wait,' said Hamid. ✔ ✔ ✔ ✔ ✔ ✔ ✔ ✔

| 'Don't worry,' gasped William, 'we can | ✔ | ✔ | (sc) said | ✔ | ✔ | ✔ |
| tell them it's an emergency.' | ✔ | ✔ | ✔ | ✔ | ✔ |

105 words
(97 words read accurately)

Levels of reading

The following reading levels can be used as a guide to match readers and books:

Independent level: A 96–100% accuracy rate. The child should have very good comprehension of the passage.

Instructional level: A 90–95% accuracy rate. The child reads some words inaccurately, but not so many that he fails to understand the passage. He can give a satisfactory answer to most questions used to test his comprehension.

Frustration level: A less than 90% accuracy rate. He may show signs of anxiety and reading aloud is laborious. He should be reading at a lower stage.

Analyzing the types of miscue a child has made

To analyze the miscues a child has made and therefore the strategies he is using you should ask yourself the following questions about every miscue: In decoding a word incorrectly, is the child using:

- the sense/meaning of the passage or sentence to decode a word? (so it makes sense in context, for example, 'when they got to the park' for 'when they reached the park')
- a knowledge of grammar or syntax to decode a word? (for instance, substituting an incorrect verb for a correct verb – 'that one was broken too.' for 'that one was wrecked too.')
- visual clues such as word shape? (for example, 'telling' for 'talking')
- phonic knowledge? – trying to 'sound out' the word.

Record what proportion of miscues were caused by which strategy in the space provided on the sheet. This will help you to assess the strategies the child needs help with.

Remember: Readers at the later stages need to read at the instructional level if their reading is to develop further. As at every other stage, discussion of miscues will help the reader understand more about the reading process.

Listening to children's reading

Reading aloud to others is a useful exercise in helping children to read with confidence and expression and gives them a better understanding of syntax and punctuation. The following strategies might be useful when developing reading aloud skills.

Using the tape recorder

This can be done when you are monitoring a child's progress using a running record or at a time convenient to both child and teacher when he would normally be reading to you. Simply suggest to the child that it would be a good idea to listen to a recording of his reading and invite participation on a shared basis. This way, you can listen to the tape together and, most importantly, the child can hear his own mistakes in an informal and non-threatening situation.

If you have time, it would be a good idea to practise or prepare the reading for a re-recording of the same passage, getting the child to improve reading performance and listening to the result.

Reading with both 'ear' and 'eye'

We do not always remember that reading with an 'inward ear' plays an important part in the reading process. Listening inwardly as we read is a skill that develops with time and practice but children's ability to listen to themselves can be improved if they are encouraged to read aloud to an audience like a performer. This does not mean a child being put in front of others; it simply means encouraging the child to read as if he or she were the teller of the story and that someone is listening to them – even if it is only a doll who is having a bedtime story.

It is therefore useful to prepare a reading occasionally, spending a little time in getting the child to read with some expression. Whether the outcome of the prepared reading is that the child reads to the headteacher, his mum, the classroom helper, a friend or a group will depend on your own judgement.

Reading in a group

Reading aloud can be shared among a small group with you sharing the reading if the children lack confidence. This can be done if you allocate small parts or sections of a passage – the speech, for example – so that certain children are given 'parts'. It is often a good idea to practise those parts so that the children read for a second time with both 'ear' and 'eye'.

Occasionally a script can be prepared, either by you or by the children themselves, and this can form the basis of a tape recording or a reading for a wider audience.

Parental involvement

Experience has shown that the *Oxford Reading Tree* works best if both parents and school work in partnership with the child. It is therefore important that parents are given as full an explanation of the story approach as possible.

Even though parents may have been helping their children through the lower stages of the *Oxford Reading Tree*, there will still be plenty of information that you can give them about helping their children become confident and fluent readers. Parents should be encouraged to read other books with and to their children, for example, books from the school or classroom library.

Parents may also like to have a general discussion on reading, or air and share particular concerns. On page 23 of this guide are a number of questions to which answers have been given. Some of these questions may be points which parents themselves raise.

The quality of the information you give about the *Oxford Reading Tree*, together with your receptiveness to the parents' concerns, will influence their view of the school and form the basis on which the reading partnership can be built.

Parents may like to see some of the range of activities and materials connected with the school's reading policy. There is a video, *Learning to read with the Oxford Reading Tree*, which is available to show at parents' evenings.

What to send home

Available from Oxford University Press are free booklets called *At home with Oxford Reading Tree: A guide for parents*. You may like to use the letter to parents which is reproduced on page 32.

Materials to send home

- a *Robins* or *Jackdaws* storybook
- copies of the relevant discussion questions

Encourage parents to use

- a notebook or a home/school record book

Dear

Your child is reading the _____ storybooks from the *Oxford Reading Tree* programme and will be bringing them home for you to read together. With the books may be suggested questions for you and your child so that you can talk about the books as you share them.

Choose a quiet time to share the book. Make sure you are both comfortable and relaxed. This may be a good time to listen if your child wants to talk about other things as well – what went on in class, or something that happened in the playground.

Ask the child questions about the book – do they know what it is about? If they have already started it, can they tell you what has already happened? Above all, enjoy the reading and make the reading sessions together a special time.

Yours sincerely

**Oxford
Reading
Tree**

ROBINS Stages 6–10

●●●

●●●

Robins and More Robins storybooks

Robins

The Dump

The old vase

William and the dog

The emergency

Kate and the sheep

The photograph

The village show

A proper bike

The holiday

The secret plans

More Robins

Max makes breakfast

The long journey

Mum's new car

The surprise

William's mistake

Treasure hunt

Hamid does his best

William and the Pied Piper

Ghost tricks

The discovery

Robins

Please read the general introductory sections of this guide before starting on this section.

What are Robins?

Robins and *More Robins* cover Stages 6 to 10 of the *Oxford Reading Tree*. The aim of the *Robins* branch is to provide a choice of enjoyable reading material for children who are rapidly growing in reading competence but who still require a story which is not too demanding in length or too difficult in concept.

The components for the *Robins* are:
  ◆ Ten *Robins* storybooks
  ◆ Ten *More Robins* storybooks
  ◆ Five *Robins* Workbooks.

The Robins stories
Stage 6 *The Dump*
Stage 7 *The old vase*
         William and the dog
Stage 8 *The emergency*
         Kate and the sheep
Stage 9 *The photograph*
         The village show
         A proper bike
Stage 10 *The holiday*
         The secret plans

The More Robins stories
Stage 6 *Max makes breakfast*
Stage 7 *The long journey*
         Mum's new car
Stage 8 *The surprise*
         William's mistake
Stage 9 *Treasure hunt*
         Hamid does his best
         William and the Pied Piper
Stage 10 *Ghost tricks*
         The discovery

They all have 32 pages.

The stories feature characters from the trunk and *Owls* storybooks – Biff, Chip, Wilf, Wilma, Nadim and

Anneena. There are also stories about completely new characters: William and Hamid; Kate and Jo; Lenny and Tracey; Ben and Laura; Max and Kerry; John and Lisa; Jess and Ann; and Amy. The stories have a variety of settings, both rural and urban.

There are also six *Catkins* and six *More Catkins* Poetry Books at Stage 5–6, and ten *Conkers* and ten *More Conkers* Poetry Books at Stage 7–8.

How do the Robins work?

Robins are designed to give children experience of a slightly more complex narrative than that of the *Owls* stories. Whilst retaining the excitement and humour characteristic of the earlier stories the *Robins* offer variety, using different characters and settings. The relationship between text and illustration is less tightly controlled, and the sentence structure, while remaining straightforward and uncluttered, is less restricted than that of the earlier stories thus allowing each *Robins* story to be written in an appropriate style.

Using the storybooks
The storybooks should be introduced to the children using the five-step approach (see page 35 and 'Putting the *Oxford Reading Tree* approach into practice', page 17).

Using the discussion questions
Use the questions provided to encourage children to talk about the characters, the plot, the storyline, incidents, feelings and emotions. This will help children to understand the reasons that lie behind what happens in any story and gain a sense of time and location.

Talking and thinking about stories and listening to what others think and say about them is central to the philosophy of the *Oxford Reading Tree*. Give the children the opportunity to share these stories with others, to talk them through and be sensitive to the questions they raise and the issues they cover.

In this guide, there are discussion questions to accompany each page of the *Robins* stories, together with detailed suggestions for general discussion; for

The five-step approach

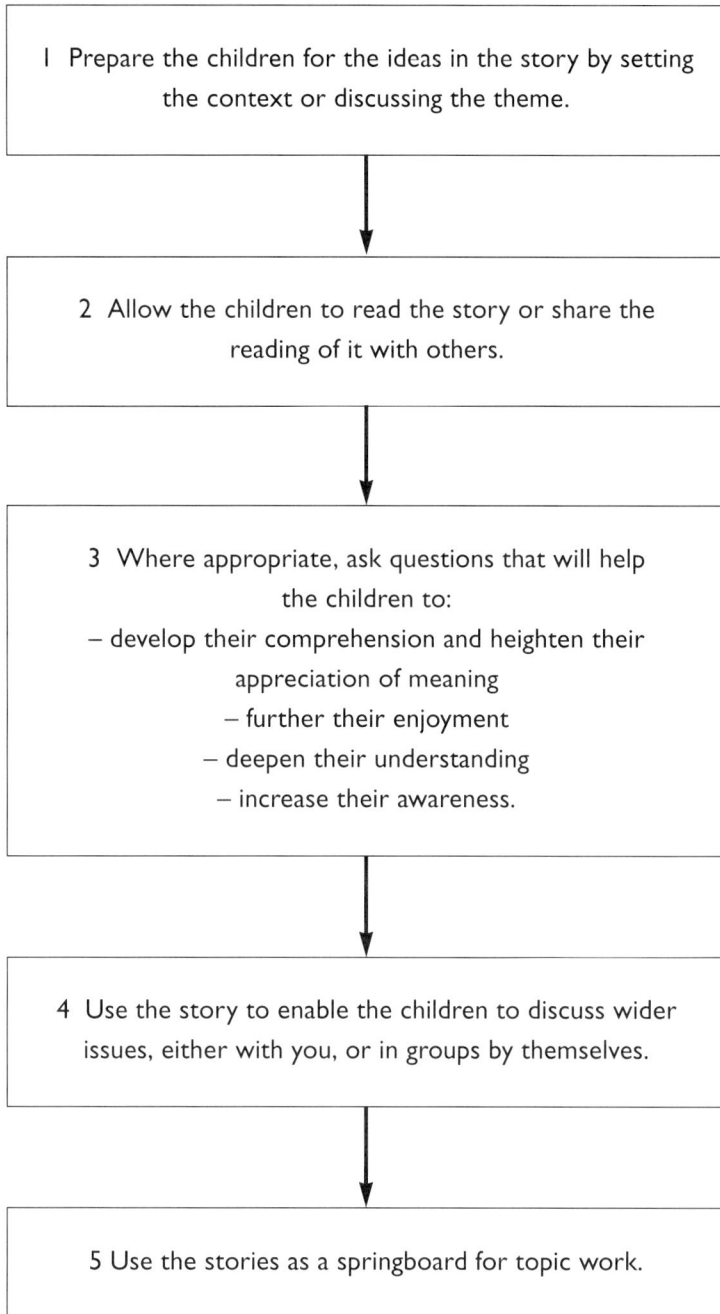

```
I  Prepare the children for the ideas in the story by setting
   the context or discussing the theme.
```

↓

```
2  Allow the children to read the story or share the
   reading of it with others.
```

↓

```
3  Where appropriate, ask questions that will help
   the children to:
   – develop their comprehension and heighten their
     appreciation of meaning
        – further their enjoyment
        – deepen their understanding
        – increase their awareness.
```

↓

```
4  Use the story to enable the children to discuss wider
   issues, either with you, or in groups by themselves.
```

↓

```
5  Use the stories as a springboard for topic work.
```

Storybook	Workbook	Stage
The Dump The old vase	Workbook 1	6/7
William and the dog The emergency	Workbook 2	7/8
Kate and the sheep The photograph	Workbook 3	8/9
The village shop A proper bike	Workbook 4	9
The holiday The secret plans	Workbook 5	10

These workbooks include activities such as cloze, sequencing, ordering, true/false, yes/no, as well as word-puzzles and simple crosswords. These reinforce the language in the *Robins* storybooks.

The comprehension exercises require reference to the relevant storybook. It is important for the children to have a copy of the storybook beside them when they are working on the workbook material.

Throughout the five workbooks some types of activities appear several times, the layout of the work often enabling pupils to identify at once the nature of an exercise without reference to the teacher. However, in order to keep the work fresh and challenging, each book introduces some new activities.

As well as word recognition the workbooks develop higher-order reading skills of empathizing, narrative voice, perspective, and develop the child's imagination by requiring the child to think up alternative endings to stories. The workbooks also require the child to write/ compose stories, at first based on visual clues such as a sequence of comic strip pictures, then one general picture.

Using the language activities
There are three photocopiable language activity sheets for each storybook, starting on page 65. These have been arranged in the same way as the discussion questions, with all activities for a particular Stage being grouped together.

The comprehension sheets are progressive, moving from answer-assisted questions at Stage 6 to literal and

More Robins there are just suggestions for general discussion. However, there is no reason why you should not ask questions of your own on a similar page-by-page basis on the *More Robins* storybooks.

These questions have been arranged in order of the Stages – for example, questions for all the Stage 9 storybooks, whether *Robins* or *More Robins*, can be found together.

Using the workbooks
There are five *Robins* workbooks which fit into the scheme as follows:

inferential questions at Stage 10. The creative writing activity sheets encourage a variety of writing skills, involving creating stories from a stimulus, writing the story portrayed in one picture or a series of pictures, creating a recipe and writing letters. The remaining language activity sheets develop a number of different language skills, including cloze procedure, sequencing, grammar, instructional writing and further comprehension work, for example, extracting information from posters and adverts.

The activities cover many aspects of the National Curriculum in England and Wales and the Scottish Office Guidelines, English Language 5-14. For grids showing specific skills/activities provided by the language activities please see page 64.

Record keeping

Page 132 provides a checklist of all the *Robins* and *More Robins* storybooks. At this stage, you may want to encourage the children to complete this themselves, so that they can record their own progress.

Assessment

There are four passages provided for *Robins* and *More Robins*. These are each about 100 words long and are designed to enable teachers to keep a running record when children are reading aloud. These passages may be found on pages 133–136. They are taken from:

Stage 6	*The Dump* (pages 20–22)
Stage 7	*The long journey* (pages 16–18)
Stage 9	*Treasure hunt* (pages 6–8)
Stage 10	*The holiday* (pages 25–27)

Each sheet has questions to assess the child's understanding of the text and ability to predict or remember what happened next.

Notes on calculating an accuracy rate are on page 27.

Discussion questions

The Dump (*Robins*)

Discussion pointers

Page 1
What sort of boy do you think Lenny is?
Do you think Lenny lives in a town or in the country?
What do you think The Dump is?
Why do you think 'Dump' has a capital D?

Pages 2/3
Why did Lenny think The Dump was a good place to play?
What sort of place is 'safe' to play in? What sort of places aren't safe?
Do you think The Dump would be a safe place for little children? Why?
If you could play there what would you like to do?
What can you see at the bottom of the ladder? Why did the children put it there?
How many tyres can you see? What sort of games could you play with tyres?

Pages 4/5
How many children have paint brushes?
Do you think that anyone would mind the children painting a picture on the wall?
Why wasn't the picture very good?
Would you like to paint a giant picture on a wall? What would you paint?

Page 6
What sort of picture did Lenny's brother and his friends paint on the wall?
Have you ever seen a picture painted on a wall? What did it look like?
Why did Lenny's brother and his friends have time to paint the picture?

Page 7
Why did the workmen come to The Dump?

What do you think was going to happen to The Dump?

Page 8
Why did the workmen say they were putting a fence round the site?
How do you think the children felt about this?

Page 9
What did the woman say the site was going to be used for?
Why did the woman have a big plan? What is a plan used for when houses are built?

Pages 10/11
Why was Lenny upset?
What did Lenny's brother tell him?
Why do children who live in towns need a special place to play?

Page 12
Why was Lenny's brother pleased about the building site?
Why did Lenny's brother not have any work to do?

Page 13
Why were Lenny and his friends 'fed up'?
What was Lenny's idea?

Pages 14/15
Why did Lenny have to write the letter three times?
What do you think Lenny hoped the Council would do?
Have you ever written a letter? Why do you always put your address at the top and sign your name at the bottom?

Pages 16/17
Why was Lenny excited?
Where were Lenny's friends playing football?
What did the letter say?
Have you ever been sent a letter? What was it about?

Pages 18/19
What sort of playground did the Council provide?
Was it a better playground than The Dump?
Why were Lenny and his friends disappointed?
What wouldn't they be able to do in the new playground that they could do at The Dump?

Which would you prefer, a playground like this one, or one like The Dump? Why?

Pages 20/21
Why did the builders put such a big fence round the building site?
Where did Lenny and his friends play?
Why isn't it a good idea to play football in the street?
How did the ball go over the fence? Have you ever kicked a ball or something over a fence? What happened?
Why wouldn't Lenny be able to get the ball?
Why shouldn't children ever play on building sites?

Pages 22/23
What did Lenny see when he looked over the fence?
What did Tracey think the men were doing?
Why did she tell Lenny to get the number of the lorry?

Pages 24/25
Do you think Lenny did the right thing when he told his brother about the men?
Why is it a good idea to tell a grown-up if you see something you think is wrong, or if you see something that worries you?
Why is stealing wrong?
What did Lenny's brother plan to do?

Pages 26/27
Why was the Boss pleased with Lenny and his friends?
When Lenny saw all the planks and pipes, it gave him an idea. What do you think the idea was?
What is a reward? Do you think Lenny and his friends deserved a reward?

Pages 28/29
How did the Boss think he could help the children?

Pages 30/31
Why do you think that things like an old lorry, planks and drums and tyres are good fun to play with?

Page 32
Why do you think Lenny and his friends were so pleased?

General discussion

The story
Did you like the story? Do you know anybody like the people in the story? Could it be a true story?
Why were Lenny and his friends upset when the workmen came to put a fence round The Dump?
Why was The Dump such a good place for Lenny and his friends to play?
Would you like to play in The Dump? What would you do there?
Why was Lenny's letter a good idea?
What mistake did the Council make when they built the new playground?
Why was it a good idea for Lenny to tell a grown-up when he saw the men doing something suspicious?

Playgrounds
What is the difference between a playground in a park and an adventure playground?
Imagine you had the money for you and your friends to make a wonderful playground. What would you put in it? How would you plan it?
How can playgrounds be dangerous? What should a safe playground be like?

*Being careful**
Why should you never go on to or play on a building site? Why are building sites dangerous?
How should you be careful if you have to play in the street or near a road?
Lenny saw some men acting suspiciously. What does that mean?
What should you always do if you see anyone acting in a suspicious way?

**Note* It would be hoped that most young children will not be in a position where they are unsupervised for long periods of play, but even so many children do have to worry about the problems of looking after themselves, or being looked after by older children.

Max makes breakfast (More Robins)

General discussion

The story
Have you ever made a birthday card for someone? Who was it for? What was it like?
Why do you think that a home-made card means more

to the person you made it for than one you could buy from a shop?

Why do you think Kerry decided to do her painting in the kitchen?

Bubbles is very special to Max. Have you got a special Ted or soft toy? Did you have one when you were younger? What was it like? Why do you think it was so special?

Kerry was very cross with Max. Do you think she was right to be so cross? Grandad wasn't cross with the children. Why do you think he wasn't cross?

Did you like the way the story finished? Do you think any of them told Mum and Dad what really happened? Dad looks puzzled on the last page. What has he noticed? What do you think might happen next?

Families/grandparents

Have you ever lived or stayed with your grandparents? Is their home very different from yours? How?

What sort of things do your grandparents like to do? What sort of music do they like to listen to? Do you like it?

Do you ever do any jobs to help your grandparents? What do you do?

Do your grandparents help you or your parents in any way?

How?

How old do you think Kerry and Max are? Do you have a younger brother or sister who is about Max's age? Do you help to look after them sometimes? Is it difficult? Some parents with children Max's age say that they need eyes in the back of their heads. What do you think this means? Would it be useful for your teacher too?

Cooking/eating

Have you ever done any cooking? At home? At school? What did you make?

The ingredients are what you make food with. Can you remember what ingredients you used?

What's your favourite meal that your mum or dad cooks?

Do you think cooking is difficult? Why?

It can be dangerous. Can you think of some rules that would be good to remember in the kitchen?

Have you ever tried any foods from different countries? (spaghetti, pizza, curry, sweet and sour?) Do you know what country they originally came from?

In Britain now we can eat a variety of foods from different countries. Have you got a take-away near you? What sort of food does it sell? Do you like it?

A lot of the food we eat can't be grown in our country and we buy it from other countries. Can you think of any? Why can't we grow it ourselves?

Painting

Do you like painting? Have you got any paints at home? What do you think was the best picture that you have ever painted?

If you want to make the colour green, what two colours do you mix? If you want to make the colour orange, what two colours do you mix? If you want to make the colour purple, what two colours do you mix? What is your favourite activity in art? (brush painting, finger painting, bubble painting, printing, collage?) Why?

Stage 7

The old vase (*Robins*)

Discussion pointers

Page 1
What do you remember about Lenny from the story 'The Dump'?
Do you have a younger brother, sister or cousin? Do you know someone who is a 'bit of a handful'? What does that mean?
How old do you think Tracey is? Is she older than Lenny? How do you know?

Pages 2/3
What sort of things do you see in antique shops?
Have you ever seen anything that is an antique? Can you say what sort of things antiques are?
For example: grandfather clock
an old gun or a sword
a very old piece of furniture
Why do you think antiques cost so much money? Why would an old vase cost seven hundred pounds?
If you had seven hundred pounds, would you spend it on an old vase? What would you spend it on?

Pages 4/5
Have you ever been to a fair or a fete at your school?
What sort of things did you see and do?
Why do schools hold things like fairs?
What sort of things do you find at a fete or fair? Do you remember any of the sideshows?
Which sideshows can you see in the picture?
If you could only go on one sideshow which one would you choose? Why?

Pages 6/7
What is a coconut shy?
Why is it hard to knock coconuts off their wooden stands?
Why did Tracey say it must be glued on?
Do you think Mel was lucky to hit the coconut off with his first ball?
Do you think Tracey liked coconut shies?

Page 8
Would you have taken the coconut or chosen one of the prizes? Why?

Page 9
Why did Lenny want Mel to take the vase?
Do you think the vase was valuable?
What is the difference between holding a vase that is worth a pound, and one that is worth seven hundred pounds?

Pages 10/11
What do you suppose Lenny was thinking as the vase sailed through the air?
Why do you think Tracey and Lenny didn't catch the vase? Are you good at catching?

Pages 12/13
Why do you think none of the children wanted to carry the vase? Would you like to carry it?
Why do you think everyone was scared of Ann Godfrey?
Do you know anyone like Ann Godfrey?
What did Lenny mean when he said he thought Ann Godfrey was looking for trouble?

Pages 14/15
Would it have been a good idea to tell Ann Godfrey that the vase was worth a lot of money?
Would Ann Godfrey have been sorry if the vase had been dropped and smashed?

Page 16
Have you ever been very angry? What is the difference between being angry and losing your temper?
Why is it a bad idea to lose your temper?
Do you need to get angry sometimes? Did Tracey need to get angry?

Page 17
Do the two vases look the same to you?

Pages 18/19
Why didn't the lady in the shop trust the children?
What did she think they might do?
What sort of shops aren't very pleased to have children?

Page 20
How was the vase in the antique shop different from the one that the children brought in?

Why did the lady take the trouble to show the valuable vase to the children?

Page 21
Why were the children so disappointed? What did they think the lady would do when they showed her their vase?
What would you do with the vase, now you know it is not worth anything?

Pages 22/23
Why do you think Lenny wouldn't tell the others what his plan was?
What do you think his plan was?

Page 24/25
Do you think Lenny's idea was a good one? Why?
Would it be easy to break the vase? Why?
Why would you like to have a go at breaking the vase on Lenny's stall?
Why is it fun to break something that doesn't matter?
Why wouldn't we break a valuable vase or good plates?

Pages 26/27
Will Lenny and Tracey make a lot of money or not very much money at this stall? Why?
What will they do once the vase has been smashed?
What do you think the teachers will say when they find out about the smashing-the-vase stall?

Pages 28/29
What does 'faint' mean when somebody says they're going to faint?
Why did the lady from the antique shop feel like fainting?

Pages 30/31
How had the vases become mixed up?
Why do you think nobody had noticed the difference?
What would the children have had to do if the valuable vase had been smashed?

Page 32
How were the children lucky in the end?
Why did the lady give them five pounds?
What do you think Mel will do to the old vase now?
What would you do?

General discussion

The story
Did you like the story? Do you think the children were lucky in the end? Decide which things in the story were lucky and which things were unlucky.
Why do you think nobody realized that the two vases had become muddled up? What would have happened if the valuable antique vase had been smashed?
What might have happened if the vase which Mel won at the coconut shy had been worth a lot of money?

Antiques
What are antiques? Have you ever seen an antique? Why do you think people like to collect antiques?
Imagine you found a gold ring and you discovered it belonged to a king or to somebody very famous who lived a long time ago. Why would the ring be valuable? Would it be less valuable if it belonged to an ordinary person once upon a time?
We all have things that matter to us. These things are precious but they are not always antiques. Do you have something at home that you wouldn't swap? Is it an antique?
Supposing you were given a gold watch that belonged to your grandfather or great-grandfather. Would you want to sell it, or would you want to keep it? Why?

Fetes and fairs
Why do schools and churches and clubs run fetes and fairs like the one in the story? Have you ever been to a fair like that one? Does your school ever run one?
What sort of stall or sideshow at a fete or a fair do you like most of all?

Bullies
What are bullies? Ann Godfrey and her gang were bullies. Why is bullying a bad thing? What should you do when a bully tries to frighten you?

William and the dog (*Robins*)

Discussion pointers

Page 1
What is William's Saturday job, and how much does he get?

Do you ever get pocket money for doing jobs at home?
What was William saving up to buy?
If you were saving up, what would you like to buy?
How do you know William isn't very good at saving up?

Pages 2/3
How old do you think William and Hamid are?
Why do you think Hamid might be better than William at saving up?
Why does Hamid want to buy a tape?
Do the boys live in a big town or a little village? How do you know?
William and Hamid go to the shopping centre by themselves. Why should children always tell a grown-up before they go somewhere by themselves?

Pages 4/5
What sort of dog is Toffee?
Why do you think Mrs Lacey likes William to take a dog like that for a long walk?
Why was Toffee a good kind of dog for an old lady to have? Why was he not a good sort of dog?
Why was it a bad idea to take a dog like Toffee to a busy shopping centre?
Do you know of any dogs like Toffee who are full of energy? What do they do?

Page 6
Why did Mrs Lacey tell William not to let Toffee off his lead until they were off the main roads?
Why is a lead a good thing for a dog?
What should you teach your dog to do so that it won't get into trouble when it is let off the lead?

Page 7
Why did William let Toffee off the lead?
Why was William being foolish to do this?

Page 8
What is the Tube? What sort of trains run in the Tube?
Do you know why they are called Tube trains? What is the other name for them?
Have you ever been on a train?
Why do you think trains run under the ground in big towns like London and Newcastle?
Would you like to go on an underground train? Why?

Page 9
Why didn't Toffee like travelling on the underground train?
What do you think Toffee is thinking?

Pages 10/11
What did Toffee do in the shopping centre which would make William think that he was a good dog?
Have you ever been to a shopping centre like the one in the picture?
What is an escalator? Have you ever been on one?
What sort of shops do you like going inside? Which ones don't you like so much?

Pages 12/13
In the cafe, why did William think he should put Toffee on his lead?
What do you think Floppy thought when he saw the poodle?
What do you think might happen next?

Pages 14/15
Describe what is happening in the picture.
How can you tell, looking at William and Hamid, that it all happened very quickly?
How would you feel if you had a dog and it did what Toffee did?
What would have happened if Toffee had not been tied to a chair in the cafe? Would the disaster have been quite as bad?

Page 16
What do you think William and Hamid thought as they were sent away from the cafe?
What do you think the waiter said to the boys?

Page 17
Why do you think William has let Toffee off the lead again? What did they agree to do at the beginning of the story?
What does the notice say about dogs?
Have William and Hamid seen the notice yet?
Why must dogs be kept on the lead in parks like this one?

Pages 18/19
Now what was Toffee up to?
Why are William and Hamid running out of the park?
What do you think the man would say if he could catch Toffee and the boys?

Pages 20/21

Why do you think Toffee wouldn't let William put him on the lead?

Why are there paintings hanging on the railing?

Pages 22/23

Toffee has run into a very posh shop. What can you see about it that shows it is different from usual food shops?

What is a manager of a shop? What is a customer?

Why shouldn't dogs be allowed to go into food shops?

Do you think William is sorry he brought Toffee with him into the town? Why?

Page 24

What do you think the shop assistant said when Toffee grabbed the fish?

Page 25

Why did Toffee wag his tail? Do you think he was pleased with himself?

What do you think the manager thought of Toffee and the boys?

What do you think William ought to say?

Page 26

Why did the lady think that Toffee was a well-behaved dog?

Page 27

What does the word 'automatic' mean?

Why couldn't William and Hamid open the doors for themselves?

Page 28

Do you think Toffee got off by mistake? What do you think he is thinking as the train moves off?

What will Mrs Lacey say if William and Hamid lose Toffee?

Page 29

What does the inspector mean when he says 'I'll phone down the line'?

What might the boys have to do to get Toffee back?

Pages 30/31

How do you know Toffee wasn't still on the platform at the other station?

Where do you think Toffee is?

Page 32

How did Toffee get back to the boys?

Would you take a dog like Toffee shopping? If you had to take him, what would you make sure to do?

General discussion

The story

Mrs Lacey was old and lived all alone. Why do you think she liked having a dog? Was Toffee a good sort of dog for an old lady to own?

What would be the best sort of dog for an old person like Mrs Lacey to own? Why do you think she liked William to take the dog for a long walk on Saturday mornings?

Do you think William and Hamid were not very sensible to take a dog like Toffee into the town? Why isn't it a good idea to take dogs into busy places?

Do you think all the things that happened in the story would happen in real life? What were the four incidents that happened as a result of Toffee misbehaving? How far do you think William was to blame?

How did Toffee manage to make his way to the next station after he had run off the underground train? Do you think a dog would have done what Toffee did? In fact, the incident on the underground did really happen to a dog and its owner.

What sort of story would you say this one is? Is it a serious story or a funny one?

Looking after dogs

Why is it important to train dogs to walk sensibly on a lead? Why is it silly to let dogs loose in the street or in busy or crowded places?

How can dogs be a nuisance to other people in streets and parks?

If a dog is let off a lead what is the one important thing that it must be trained to do?

How intelligent do you think dogs are? What sort of things can they be trained to do? What are guide dogs for blind people? What are police dogs and sniffer dogs? Can you think of other ways in which dogs help people? Have you ever heard of working dogs? What do they do?

What does obedient mean? Why is it important for a dog to be obedient? Why wasn't Toffee an obedient dog?

Shopping centres

Have you ever been to a shopping centre? Was it like

the one in the story? Why are shopping centres that are under cover nicer than ones that are out in the open air? What did Hamid and William have to do before they went off to the shopping centre? Why is it important even for big children to tell their parents or a grown-up where they are going?

Saving up

What was Hamid carrying with him in the story? Why wasn't it a good idea to take an expensive radio into a big town?

How much had William saved towards his computer? Do you think that Hamid was better at saving up his money? If you had any money what would you save it for?

The long journey (More Robins)

General discussion

The story

Did you like the way the story ended? Why? Why not? Did you guess that Grandad would come to the rescue? Why?

Why had Grandad decided not to go on holiday with the family?

Why did Dad say it was 'a bit of luck' when Max fell asleep in the car almost at once?

Where was the cottage? Do you know where Devon is? Have you ever been to Devon?

Dad looks worried a lot during the story. What is he worrying about?

When they get to the cottage, Mum is rather cross with Dad. Why? Mum feels cross with herself later. Why?

Why couldn't they go to a cafe for tea?

What sort of things did Kerry pack in her bag for her holiday?

What was the most important thing that Max wanted to take with him?

Do you think that after that awful start they had a good holiday? Why?

Journeys

Have you ever been stuck in a traffic jam? Why do you think people sometimes get bad tempered when they are in a traffic jam?

Have you ever been to a service station? You cannot

stop your car on a motorway so it is very important to have service stations. What are they like? What can you do there?

When you go on a long journey, what do you like to do in the back of the car? Do you go to sleep? listen to the radio or tapes? play guessing games? play 'I spy'? Why isn't it a good idea to read? Do you get bored sometimes?

Do you sometimes feel car sick? What do you do to feel better?

Have you ever noticed when there are road works, there are a lot of cones along the road. What are they used for? Why do you think they are red and white? What does the road sign on page 12 mean?

Holidays

Have you been on a long journey on holiday? Where did you go? What did you take with you to do in the car? What did you pack in your case? Who does the packing in your family? Have you ever forgotten anything important? What did you do?

Have you ever started a journey really early like Kerry's family to try to avoid the traffic? What is it like very early in the morning? What is different?

Has it ever rained a lot when you were on holiday? What did you do when it rained?

Have you ever been on holiday with your grandparents? What do you like to do at the seaside? What do your grandparents like to do at the seaside?

Brothers and sisters

Have you got a little brother or sister? Max is still learning to talk. How can you tell that he is young from the way that he talks?

When you were little did you have funny names for words you found difficult to say? What were they? Does your younger brother or sister use some unusual words?

Mum's new car (More Robins)

General discussion

The story

What was Mum's job? Do you know a nurse? Do you think that being a nurse is a difficult job? Why? Why not? What do they have to do?

Why did Mum need a new car? Why do you think Lisa

was so fond of the old car? What were they going to have to do without in order to have a new car?

Why do you think some of the cars in the showroom could be called 'old bangers'? What is an 'old banger'? Why is it called that?

Why was Mum so sure that the car would be safe in the multi-storey car park?

Look at the expressions on the faces of Mum and Lisa on page 16. What do you think they are feeling?

Did you think that the man looked suspicious?

How do you think Mum felt when she realized her mistake?

How do you think the wedding cake turned up at the police station? What do you think had happened?

Was Aunt Vicky upset about going to church in the old car? Why not?

Cars

Have your family got a car? What sort of car is it? Is it old? Is it new? Have you had the car so long that like Lisa you feel it is part of the family?

Has your car ever broken down? What did you do?

Some people pay money each year to a breakdown service which will come and help them if they break down. Do you think it is a good idea? Do you know the name of any? (You may have seen adverts for them on the television.)

Do you know how old you have to be before you can drive a car? There are some important rules that you need to know before you can drive a car. They are in a book. Do you know what it is called?

Have your parents bought a car recently? Did you go with them? Was it exciting? If you could have any type of car, what car would you like?

Weddings

What is a wedding? Have you ever been to one? What was it like?

Have you ever been a bridesmaid or a page-boy? How did you feel? What did you wear?

What sort of clothes do people wear at weddings? What sort of places do people usually go to to get married?

After the wedding people take lots of photographs. Why? Why do you think people wear and carry flowers at a wedding?

People do lots of things at a wedding because it is the tradition. What do you think a 'tradition' is?

Do you have some traditions in your family (for example, at Christmas or birthdays)?

Stage 8

The emergency (*Robins*)

Discussion pointers

Page 1
Do you know what an emergency is? (Think of an easy example such as a water pipe bursting in the classroom, or a tiger coming into the playground!) What has to happen when there is an emergency?
What did William mean when he said 'Toffee won't get away from us now'?★ Why does Toffee look so miserable?
What does William think is clever about his idea of the long rope?
★See *William and the dog*

Page 2
Do you remember whose dog Toffee was?★
What does William do every Saturday?★
Why it is important to train dogs to go on a lead?
★See *William and the dog*

Page 3
What did the boys think when Mrs Lacey didn't come to the door?
How old is Mrs Lacey?
What might be wrong with her?

Pages 4/5
How do you know that Toffee thought something was wrong?
What do you think had happened to Mrs Lacey?
Why do old people sometimes fall over?
Why was this an emergency?

Page 6
Why do neighbours sometimes have keys to each other's houses?
Why is it a good thing to have a friendly neighbour?
How do you know that Mrs Knight or Mrs Lacey didn't have a phone?

Page 7
What do we call the sort of person who breaks a telephone?

Why is it a very bad thing that a public telephone is smashed?

Pages 8/9
What has happened to the box outside the cinema?
What do you think should happen to people who smash things like telephone boxes?

Pages 10/11
How old do you think the two boys are who have set fire to the telephone books?
Do you think these two boys might have damaged the other broken boxes? Why?
Why are the two boys running away?

Page 12
The fire in the phone box is an emergency too. Which emergency was the more urgent – putting out the fire, or phoning for the ambulance? Why?

Page 13
How do you know that Hamid's shop was a long way from Mrs Lacey's house?

Pages 14/15
Where is the ambulance taking Mrs Lacey?
Why do broken telephone boxes put people's lives in danger?

Pages 16/17
Have you ever been in a hospital? Have you ever visited anyone in hospital?
Why do people need to go to hospital?
How was Mrs Lacey when the boys went to visit her?
Why didn't they take Toffee in to see her?

Pages 18/19
Which box is the telephone engineer mending?
Why does the engineer get fed up?
What would happen if there weren't people like the engineer to mend things?

Pages 20/21
What sort of boys were Toby Keene and Jim Bowman?
Why were Hamid and William frightened of them?
Have you ever met a bully? What did the bully do?

Page 22
Why did William wish he had Toffee with him?

What can you do about bullies? What is the best thing to do if you meet them? Is it a good idea to tell somebody about them? Whom should you tell? What do you think Toffee would say to William if he could speak?

Pages 24/25
Why is it lucky that William and Hamid are behind the bushes in the park?
What do you think Toby and Jim are doing?
What would you do if you were William and Hamid?

Page 26
What sort of dog had Toffee seen?
When was the last time Toffee had chased a poodle?★
What makes you think that Toffee doesn't like poodles?
What do you think is going to happen next?
★See *William and the dog*

Page 27
Why was it lucky that the rope wound round the telephone box?
What would you do now?

Pages 28/29
Why hadn't Toby and Jim seen William and Hamid?
Why did William tie up the ends of the rope?
What happened next? Why was that lucky for William and Hamid?

Pages 30/31
What did Toby and Jim plan to do to the mended telephone box?
What do you think would have happened if the two bullies had seen William and Hamid?
What does to be 'caught red-handed' mean?
Toby and Jim began to cry. What does that tell you about bullies?
Do you feel sorry for Toby and Jim?

Page 32
What did William mean when he said that Toffee was no bother except to Toby and Jim?
Do you think Mrs Lacey was interested in what happened when Toffee caught the boys in the telephone box?

General discussion

The story
Did you learn anything from this story? Would you ever do what Toby and Jim did to a public telephone?
Do you think the story had a good ending? Do you think people who do bad things usually get caught in the end?
Do you think Toffee knew that he had helped to catch the vandals?
How were William and Hamid lucky?
Did you feel sorry for Jim and Toby at the end of the story, or did you think they got what they deserved?

Emergencies
Luckily Mrs Lacey was only suffering from a bad fall. What might have happened if she had been seriously ill, or had hurt herself badly?
Why is it important to have telephones that work?
Talk about how to use a telephone in an emergency. Could you make an emergency call? Why would it be a good idea to learn how to make an emergency call?
Can you think of any situations when you might need to make an emergency call?

Vandalism
What would you say to Toby Keene and Jim Bowman if you could tell them off?
Do you think William and Hamid would ever vandalize a telephone box?
What else is broken or damaged by vandals? Why is vandalism such a problem and a nuisance?

Emergency services
What else comes along when there is an emergency, apart from an ambulance? Would you like to be a fireman or an ambulance driver? Why?
Have you ever seen an emergency – a fire, or an accident in the street? What happened?

Old people
Why is it a good thing to make friends with a neighbour who is old and lives alone?
Do you know any old people like Mrs Lacey? Who are they?

People who mend things
In the story a telephone engineer mended the broken telephones.

Who else mends things? What is the name of the person who mends the following?

water pipes and taps
wooden things
electrical things
window glass
motor cars
shoes

People who help us
In the story, Mrs Lacey was taken to hospital by the ambulance crew. Who else helps us? What other jobs can you think of where people help others?

Kate and the sheep (*Robins*)

Discussion pointers

Page 1
Why doesn't Kate think that Solomon is much of a pet?
Dad looks a bit cross. Why do you think that is?
Why is it a bad idea to allow animals to jump on to a table where food is eaten?
Why would it be serious if a dog were to chase a sheep?
How old do you think Kate and Jo are?

Pages 2/3
The lady in the shop looks a bit cross. Why do you think that is?
Why isn't it a good idea to have dogs in a shop where food is served?
What sort of dog is Gyp?
What is a ewe?
What sort of dog do you think Glenn is?

Pages 4/5
Why do sheep sometimes have to be moved from one field to another?
Mr Munday was teasing the girls. How? Do sheep have meal times?
How does Glenn help his master?

Pages 6/7
Why did Mr Munday say he needed all the help he could get?
What does lambing mean?
At what time of the year does lambing start?

Pages 8/9
What did Mr Munday mean when he said Glenn wasn't a pet but a working dog?
What is the difference between a pet and a working dog?
Can you name five or six other animals that work?
Could any animal work? Could you have a working crocodile or a working goldfish? Why not?

Pages 10/11
What do you think should be done about the cat?
Kate and Jo like helping. What sort of jobs do you like to do in the house?

Pages 12/13
Why was Kate's idea not a good one?
What do you think will happen if Kate and Jo let the sheep out?

Pages 14/15
Why wouldn't the sheep come when Kate called them?
Why does Jo wish they had Glenn with them?

Pages 16/17
What do you think was Kate's plan when she went up to the old ewe?
What will sheep usually do once one of them starts to move?

Pages 18/19
Why couldn't Kate and Jo control the flock?
Why was it a serious and silly thing to do to let the sheep out of the field?
Do you think Mr Mudge helped, or did he make matters worse? Why?

Pages 20/21
Why is it harder to control sheep once they have scattered?
This picture is to make you laugh. Where have some of the sheep gone? Would they really go there?

Pages 22/23
Why is a dog better than people at rounding up straying sheep?
Why was Mum cross?

Pages 24/25
Why should you say how sorry you are when you have done something wrong?
What might have happened to one of the sheep? Do you think Kate and Jo were lucky nothing did happen?

Page 26

Why was there a new-born lamb in the kitchen?

Why do some new-born lambs need to be looked after?

Page 27

Why does this lamb need to be looked after?

Why can't Mr Munday look after the lamb?

Why had Mr Munday decided to let the girls look after a lamb rather than be cross with them for letting the sheep out?

Pages 28/29

Would you like to look after a little lamb like this one?

Pages 30/31

Why wouldn't it be a good idea for the girls to get too fond of the little lamb?

Why can't an animal like a lamb ever become a pet?

Page 32

What very important lessons had the girls learned?

General discussion

The story

Nobody was pleased with Kate and Jo for letting the sheep out of the field. How do you think Kate and Jo felt when they realized they had caused so much trouble?

Mr Munday could have been very cross indeed. Instead, he gave Kate and Jo a lamb to look after. Do you agree with what he did? Shouldn't the girls have got into trouble and been punished, or did Mr Munday have a reason?

Why do you think that children who live in the country wouldn't have done what Kate and Jo did?

Sheep

Sheep are not very intelligent animals. When one sheep does something, what do others tend to do?

Why do farmers keep sheep? What do sheep provide?

What is the name of the person who looks after the sheep all the year round? Why is the life of a shepherd quite hard if the sheep graze in the mountains?

What does a sheepdog do? Why do sheepdogs have to be very intelligent and obedient?

How can stray dogs be a danger to sheep? What is sheep worrying?

Why do people have to keep dogs on a lead when walking near sheep?

The country code

Kate and Jo were trying to help when they let the sheep out of the field. What is the danger to animals if they stray out of their fields?

Why is it important to shut gates behind you?

What happens to crops like wheat and barley if people walk or run through them? Why is it important to keep to the footpaths around fields?

Why is litter, especially things like cans, glass bottles, and plastic bags, a danger to animals? How else can litter be a nuisance or a danger?

Why should animals not be frightened or chased?

The surprise (*More Robins*)

General discussion

The story

Did you enjoy reading this story? What did you think of the ending? Did you expect them to find Lucky in the boot? What did you think had happened to Lucky? Ben must find it difficult sometimes having to get around in his wheelchair or be carried. Would you find it frustrating do you think? What would you find difficult to do?

Ben's sister, Laura, is a great help. Do you think that you would be as helpful if your brother or sister had to use a wheelchair? How could you help?

Dad said that the flats were old and when they were built nobody thought about wheelchairs. Nowadays it has been made a little easier for 'disabled' people. What have you noticed in your nearest town which is to help disabled people? Is your school suitable for someone in a wheelchair? How could you make your school easier for a person in a wheelchair?

Why did Dad decide to have both kittens?

What do you think Dad meant by 'Animals aren't toys. You must think of them as new members of our family.'?

Why did Ben not want to go to his Aunty Val's and Uncle Keith's?

How did Uncle Keith try to cheer him up?

Why was it lucky that they found Lucky in the car in such a short time? What could have happened? Why?

Pets

Have you got a pet? What is it? What is it called?

What is good about having a pet? What is difficult

about having a pet?

What sort of pets do people keep? Do you know of any unusual ones?

What must you do to look after a pet? What do they need?

What do you think is the easiest pet to look after? Why?

Who has the job of feeding and cleaning your pet? Is it Mum or Dad or all of you?

What is the most common pet in your class/group?

What can you do to help make sure that you don't lose your pet or if you do, find it quickly?

The R.S.P.C.A. is the Royal Society for the Prevention of Cruelty to Animals. People who work for them try to make sure that people look after their pets properly. They use a saying 'A puppy is for life not just for Christmas'. What do you think this means?

Why do you think cats are such ideal pets for elderly people who live alone?

If you could have any pet you liked what would you have?

Losing things

Have you ever lost a pet? What did you do?

Do you often lose things at home? How do you feel if you can't find something? What do you do?

Do Mum and Dad ever lose things like keys, glasses or handbags? Does it make them cross?

What could you do to help to stop losing things so often?

William's mistake (More Robins)

General discussion

The story

Did you like this story? What did you like best? Did you have a favourite illustration? Why did you like this one best?

Why do you think William kept refusing to go out with his friends?

William likes to joke. Can you remember any funny things that he said in the story?

Why did Mum think that William was not very good at sports? Do you think she was right?

What did Tom and Emma say to William that was rather cruel? How did William feel?

Do you think that they were right to say what they did? If you had been William sitting in the tree, would you have thought you'd seen a kidnapping? Would you have

done what William did? Why? Why not?

Do you think that William is a good runner after all? Why?

How did Toffee feel after all the running?

Why did William say that he wanted to be a cameraman when he grew up?

Sports day at school

Have you ever been in a sports day at your school? Did you enjoy it? What race were you in? Did you find it difficult?

How did you feel just before the race? How did you feel when the race had finished?

How does it feel to come first in a race? How does it feel to come last in a race?

There is a saying – 'It's not the winning or the losing that's important but the taking part'. What do you think it means?

We are all good at different things, but it can feel very bad if you lose a sports race or a game. What could you say to cheer up a friend who has just lost a race or a game?

Keeping fit

In the story a number of different ways of keeping fit are mentioned. What are they? (running, football, swimming, flying a kite and walking a dog)

What do you do to keep fit? Why is keeping fit important? Where is your nearest swimming pool, park, sports centre? What else can you do to keep your body healthy besides keeping fit?

Does anyone in your family like to keep fit? What do they do?

Do you have a favourite sport that you like to watch? Does your mum or dad?

Television programmes

Do you like to watch the television? What is your favourite programme? Why?

Does your mum or dad have a favourite programme that they don't like to miss?

Look at the people making the television programme on page 29. They are called the television or production crew. What jobs do you think they are all doing?

Some programmes are filmed in a studio. Do you know where your nearest television studio is? Do you know any programmes that are made there?

This film is not being made in a studio. They say it is being filmed 'on location'. What problems could there be filming outside or in a town?

Stage 9

The photograph (*Robins*)

Discussion pointers

Page 1

In what way was William being naughty?

Why is it naughty to shout out? What should William have done if he wanted to ask a question?

What do you think had caused the damp patch on the ceiling?

Page 2

Why would the children have to work in the Hall?

Do you know why a damp patch near a light could be dangerous?

What does 'redecorate' the classroom mean?

Would you like to have your classroom repainted? Would you keep the colours the same or would you change them? What colours would you choose?

Page 3

What did William mean by 'a good laugh'? Did it mean he thought he could be naughty?

Why might it be easy for him to be naughty in the Hall?

Pages 4/5

What do we learn about in history? What is a history project?

Mrs Patel told the class that things change. Can you think of something that has changed over the years? How about aeroplanes, cars, the way people wash clothes?

Why don't people today wear the same sort of clothes that were worn a hundred or two hundred years ago?

How are the clothes in the pictures different from the ones people wear today?

Page 6

How was William being naughty?

Why is it wrong to tell jokes when you should be working?

Why is it wrong to make a noise or laugh loudly when you should be quiet?

Why is it better to be quiet when you are working?

Page 7

Can you think of two reasons why Mrs Patel was annoyed with William?

What would you say to William if you were Mrs Patel?

Pages 8/9

Why did Mrs Patel write a note to William's mum?

Why did William not want to give his mum the note?

Why was William's mum cross with him?

How are the other children in the picture being naughty? Why shouldn't children run in school, especially when they leave a room?

Pages 10/11

Why is William being silly even after his mum has been cross with him?

What does 'William's mum was not amused' mean? Do you think it means that she told William off for being cheeky?

What did William's mum mean when she said 'the old days'? Did she mean when she was at school, or did she mean long before that?

Was it a good idea to give children the cane? Do you think that William deserved the cane for being naughty in Mrs Patel's class?

Pages 12/13

How do you know that William doesn't like reading books much?

What is homework?

Do you have an older brother or sister who does homework?

Have you ever done homework? What did you do?

What did you like about doing homework and what didn't you like?

Pages 14/15

What would it be like if you had to move everything out of your classroom into the Hall?

Why was it interesting to find old school books and photographs?

Find out how old your school is.

What differences are there between an old school and a modern one?

Page 16

Do you watch Saturday morning television? What is your favourite programme?

How do you feel when someone turns off a programme that you are enjoying?

Why did Julie turn off the television?

Page 17

Do you ever visit a library? What do you do there?

Why is a library useful when you want to do a project?

Pages 18/19

Why was William so surprised at the photograph of his school?

How has the school changed? Why doesn't it have chimneys now? What do the chimneys tell you about the way the schools were heated in the past?

How did William think his classroom was different?

What is the difference between a desk and a table?

Why didn't the children have television in school in those days?

Did your parents have a television in school? How about your grandparents?

Page 20

What picture was William looking at?

Page 21

What has happened? Whose is the angry voice?

Do you think William is having a dream?

Pages 22/23

Why do you think the children in the picture look unhappy?

How is the teacher in the picture different from your teacher?

How is the old classroom different from a modern one?

What is an ink pen? Do children in your school use ink pens?

What is a blot?

Pages 24/25

William is quite a naughty boy. Why do you think he was too scared to say anything?

Would you be frightened of a teacher like that? Why?

Why wasn't there a sound in the classroom? Do you work without making a sound? Why is it good to be quiet sometimes?

Why did the children have to dip their pens into ink-wells?

Page 26

What was the punishment for each blot in the copybook?

What is blotting paper?

Page 27

What is the strange box on legs?

Why are the children being told to line up?

Pages 28/29

Have you ever been in a group and had your photograph taken? Who were you with? Did you smile?

Why didn't the fierce teacher tell the children to smile?

Why do you think the fierce teacher never smiled?

Page 30

Why wouldn't William like to have gone to school in those days?

Would you have liked to go to a school like that?

What is a nightmare?

What is a day-dream?

Page 31

Why was William's story so good?

Page 32

Was the boy in the picture really William, or did he just look like him?

Why was it impossible for the boy to be William?

Is it possible to go back in time?

If you could go back in time for an hour or so, what time in history would you choose? Why?

General discussion

The story

What happened to William as he was reading the book about his school in the old days? Was he dreaming, or did he really travel back in time?

If he was dreaming, how did a boy who looked like William appear on the old photograph?

What do you think William learned from the dream?

Why do you think he might be a little less naughty after the experience?

Why was Mrs Patel a good teacher? Did she try to make the work interesting for the children? Why did she have to write to William's mum? Was she right to make him take his work home?

Schools a long time ago
Look at the picture on pages 22/23. In what ways is the classroom in the picture different from your classroom? Why do you think teachers used the cane in those days? Would you?
Can you think of some of the things that schools didn't have all those years ago? What about heating or lighting? Why didn't schools have televisions, computers, and radios in those days?
Why couldn't the children write in biro or fibre-tip pen? What were ink-wells? What do you think it would be like to write with a dip pen and ink?

Punishment
What is a punishment? Have you ever been punished? Why did the fierce teacher in the story have a cane? What makes children behave themselves? Do you behave yourself when you are working?
When do you behave really well? When are you naughty?

The village show (Robins)

Discussion pointers

Page 1
Does Kate live in a town or village? How do you know? What do we call things like onions and beetroot? Which is your favourite vegetable? Which one don't you like?
Why are vegetables good for you?

Page 2
Why do people enter things in a show?
Why do you think Mum called the beetroots her 'prize beetroots'?
What is special about a 'prize-winning' vegetable?

Page 3
What are elderberries? Find out what they look like. Why don't people grow them?
What is a dandelion? Which part of the dandelion is used to make wine?
Why is wine a drink for grown-ups only? Why don't children drink it?

Pages 4/5
Why did Kate decide to make dandelion wine? What sort of things can children enter for a competition? Have you ever been in a competition on holiday, or at home? Talk about it.

Pages 6/7
Did the girls go to see Mrs Mudge as soon as they had their idea? How do you know?
Why wouldn't Mrs Mudge tell the girls how to make her wine?

Pages 8/9
Why did Kate not want to ask Mum how to make dandelion wine?
What part of the dandelions did the girls pick? What do you call the other parts of a dandelion plant?

Pages 10/11
What is a recipe? How does a recipe help you to make something?
How do you know Kate doesn't have a recipe for making dandelion wine?
What things have you made to eat or drink?

Page 12
How did Kate know that sugar is important? Had she seen anyone make wine before?
What are wine gums?
Why do you think they aren't made from wine?

Page 13
Have you ever made anything like Jo and Kate's mixture? What was it? What do you think Jo's wine will taste like?
Why doesn't this mixture seem as bad as Kipper's cake in *The toys' party*? (Stage 2)

Pages 14/15
Why did Kate have to get the dandelions out of the liquid?

Pages 16/17
Why did Kate decide to put paint in the wine?
What do you think the mixture tasted like?

Page 18
What are corks?
Why did Jo and Kate need them?
What do you use to get a cork out of a bottle?

Have you ever tried to put a cork back in a bottle? Why doesn't it fit?

Page 19
Why wasn't Mrs Mudge pleased to see Kate and Jo?
Why didn't Mrs Mudge let the girls have some corks?

Pages 20/21
Why did Mr Mudge laugh?
Why wasn't the girls' wine like Mrs Mudge's?

Page 22
What did Mr Mudge do in the cellar?

Page 23
What do you think was Mr Mudge's reason for giving the wine to the girls?
Whom did he hope would enjoy it?

Pages 24/25
Why were the girls fed up?

Pages 26/27
Why was Mum surprised when she sipped the girls' wine?
What do you think everyone thought when they realized there was real dandelion wine in the bottles?

Pages 28/29
Which bunch of carrots do you think won the prize?
Why would it be harder to judge the marrows?

Pages 30/31
Why did Mrs Mudge look pleased with herself?
Why did the judges pull nasty faces?

Page 32
Why was Mrs Mudge so cross? What do you think she said?
Why did Mr Mudge wink at the girls? Why was he pleased that Mrs Mudge hadn't won the prize for once? Do you think you should feel sorry for Mrs Mudge?

General discussion

The story
What is boasting or showing off? Why is it important not to boast or show off when you win something?

What is the difference between being pleased when you win and showing off about it?
How did Mrs Mudge behave?
Why is a competition not much fun if you know that the same person is going to win it each time?
Do you think that Mr Mudge knew that the bottle his wife would enter for the show would be one which contained Kate's mixture?
Was it a good thing that Mrs Mudge didn't win for once? Was it fair of Mr Mudge to do what he did? Would it be fair to trip someone up in a race if they were always winning it? What do you think Mrs Mudge might have said to Mr Mudge after the competition?

Competitions
Have you ever entered a competition or been in a race or taken part in a fancy dress contest? Talk about it. Why is it important not to mind if you lose? How important is it to try to win? What sports or games can you think of where people play to win? Can you think of any you play, which involve winning?
Do you like to win? Do you mind losing?

Making things
What food or drinks have you helped to make? What do you do to help your mum or dad in the kitchen? Why mustn't you make something without asking a grown-up first?

A proper bike (*Robins*)

Discussion pointers

Page 1
Do you have a bicycle? What sort do you have?
How did Anneena feel when she saw Wilma's present?
When have you felt like Anneena?

Pages 2/3
What do you give your best friend when it is his or her birthday?
Wilma's birthday treat is to have a picnic with her friends. When it is your birthday what special things do you do?
Why did Anneena feel sad?

Pages 4/5

Why wouldn't Anneena's little bike be any good on the picnic?

Do you think Wilma should have a picnic party if one of her best friends can't come? What sort of party could she have instead?

Pages 6/7

What did Anneena mean by a proper bike?

Why was she so pleased with her grandfather?

Page 8

Have you ever had some good news to tell to a friend? What was it?

How should you feel when somebody tells you some good news about themselves?

Why do you think Wilma is pleased at Anneena's news?

Page 9

How do you feel when you 'can't wait' for something to happen?

When was the last time you really looked forward to something?

Pages 10/11

How did Anneena feel when she saw the bike her grandfather had 'done up' for her? Why do you think Grandfather was pleased with himself?

How would you feel about riding a bike like that?

Why did Anneena say the bike was lovely?

Anneena didn't really think it was lovely. Was she telling the truth? Was she right to do so?

Pages 12/13

Why was Anneena surprised once she rode the bike?

Why did Chip say the bike must have come from a museum?

Pages 14/15

What do you think of the old bike? Do you like it? What do you like about it?

What did the butcher use the bike for? Do you think the butcher delivered the meat himself? Who did?

What did Wilma's mum think of the old bike?

Pages 16/17

Why didn't they cycle to the forest? Why was it a good idea to bring the bikes by car?

How was Chip being a little unkind?

Have you ever been in a big forest? What was it like?

Pages 18/19

Why did everyone have to carry something? How did the children carry the picnic things?

How was Anneena's bike proving useful?

What did Anneena offer to do?

Page 20

How was Wilma being unkind?

Why isn't it a good thing to 'show off'?

Do you think you ever show off? What do you think of others who do?

Page 21

After cycling for a time how did Biff, Chip and Wilma feel?

Page 22

Why did Anneena want to laugh?

What did she say to get her own back on the others because they had laughed at her old bike?

Page 23

When have you ever felt tired and fed up like Wilma?

Why didn't Anneena feel tired? What does that tell you about her big old bike?

Page 24

Why did they prefer to play by the lake, rather than cycle further?

Page 25

Why did Wilma's mum think that it would be a good idea for Anneena to ride Wilma's bike for a little way?

Pages 26/ 27

What happened to Wilma? What lesson did she learn about showing off?

Pages 28/29

Why wasn't Wilma's mum cross with Wilma?

How do you think Wilma felt when she realized what she had done?

What do you think Anneena's idea is?

Page 30

If they hadn't had a bike with a carrier what do you think they would have done?

Page 31

How did Wilma get her bike back?

Why did everyone feel sad?

Page 32

What did Anneena mean when she said the old bike was 'a proper bike'?

General discussion

The story

Do you think Wilma, Biff and Chip meant to be unkind to Anneena?

Why was Anneena surprised and disappointed when she saw the old bike her grandfather had done up for her? Anneena told her grandfather that the old bike was lovely. Was she right to tell a fib?

How did the old bike turn out to be a good bike after all?

How did Wilma spoil her birthday treat?

Birthday treats

How do you celebrate your birthday? Do you have a birthday treat? What sort of treat do you have?

Would you rather have lots of friends to a birthday party, or just one or two friends and do something special? Why?

What sort of things do you like to do at parties?

Outings

Would you like to go for a picnic or a cycle ride in a forest? What is there to do in a forest?

What outings have you been on?

Where did you go? What was it like?

Picnics

If you could have a picnic a) by a nice river, b) in a forest, c) on a hill with a lovely view, d) on an island in a lake, e) at the seaside, f) on a farm – which one would you choose? Why?

Showing your feelings

The story had a lot to say about people's feelings or about the way they behaved. How do you think everyone in the story felt? Here are some examples:

a) Wilma felt pleased because she had a new bike for her birthday.

b) Anneena felt sad because she didn't have a bike.

c) Anneena's grandfather felt happy because ... Think of as many as you can and talk about some of them.

Treasure hunt (*More Robins*)

General discussion

The story

Would you have liked to have gone to Grondale Hall that day?

What would you have chosen to do first?

The boys saw a poster about the open day. Posters can tell you about special events and what's on. Have you seen any posters like this one? Where was it? What was it for?

We can't see all of the poster. Is there anything that you or your parents would need to know about that day that you can't see on the poster?

What did the clue say? Read the clue aloud again. Two of the words look different but sound like each other. Which words are they? We say that these two words 'rhyme.' Can you think of any more words that rhyme?

The boys were lucky that P.C. Stocks was passing when they shouted for help. What could have happened if he hadn't heard them shout?

Did you like the way the story ended?

Were you glad that Toby and Jim didn't keep the prize?

Do you think that William was glad that Hamid had persuaded him to visit Grondale Hall?

Have you ever been surprised about a visit which turned out to be a lot better than you expected it to be?

Bullies

What is bully? Have you ever met one?

What would you do if you were being bullied at school or by children who lived near you?

What would you do if you met them in the street?

It's good to tell someone about it. Who could you tell if you were being bullied?

Special houses (stately homes)

Have you ever visited an old house or hall? Can you remember what it was called and what it was like? How was it different from your home?

The furniture in the room on pages 10 and 11 is old furniture. How can you tell that it is old? Is there anything else in the room that looks old?

Look at the statue on page 17. Lots of statues have been made of this little boy. It is an imaginary boy called Cupid. Do you know anything about Cupid? Have you seen pictures of him anywhere else?

Can you think of any rules that are important to remember if you're visiting an old house or hall? Many of the pictures that were stolen were portraits. Do you know what a portrait is? Have you ever seen one?

Grondale Hall would be a good place to take friends or family who came to stay with you. If some friends or family came to stay with you at your home, where could you take them to visit? What interesting places are there near your home?

People who help us

In the story P.C. Stocks helps to catch the thief and arrests him. Who else helps us? How do they help us? Would you like to do a job when you're older where you help others? What sort of job would you like to do?

Balloons

A hot air balloon was the first way that people were able to fly in the sky. How else can people fly now? Have you ever been in an aeroplane? Did you like it? How did you feel?

How do you think a balloon works? How does it rise up and stay up in the air? (The cylinders in the picture contain propane gas [stored as a liquid]. When the burner is lit, this gas will fill the balloon with hot air which is lighter than the surrounding air. This rises and takes the basket up into the air.)

Balloons are often used to study the weather. How do you think that they can help?

Would you like to go for a balloon ride? Why? Why not? Do you know what a bird's eye view of something is?

Hamid does his best (More Robins)

General discussion

The story

Did you enjoy the story? Which part did you like best? Did you wish that Hamid's team had won or do you think that this was a better ending? Why?

Why wouldn't Hamid give up in the football match and

tell them how ill he was feeling?

Look on pages 14 and 15 at the words that Hamid said in the play. Look at the end of the lines. Some of the words sound the same. We call it rhyming. Which words rhyme? How do you think Hamid's mum felt when he walked on to the stage dressed as the Pied Piper? And when he rushed off the stage?

Why did Hamid's team cheer him at the end of the game?

What did the doctor say was the matter with Hamid? Do you think Hamid was a brave boy? Why?

School plays

Have you ever been in a school play or class assembly? What did you have to do? Did you enjoy it? Did you wear a special costume? Did you have to learn some words or a song?

Can you remember any of what you had to say or sing? What was it?

When you saw your parents or other children from the school watching you, did you feel nervous?

Do you find it hard to speak very loud so that everyone can hear you? Is it harder when you are nervous? Have you ever sung or played an instrument in front of others? Was it fun? Was it difficult?

Football

Do you like football? Do you have a favourite football team? What are they called? What colour strip do they wear? Do you have a favourite player? What is he called? What is the name of your local team? What colour strip do they wear? Do you know the names of any of the players?

Do any members of your family ever go to a football match? Have you ever been? Would you like to go one day?

How would you describe how to play football to someone who has never heard of the game?

What do footballers wear for a football match? Why do they have studs on the bottom of their football boots?

Why do goalkeepers wear different colours from the rest of the players? What else do they wear that is different? Why?

Feeling ill

Have you ever felt really poorly? Did you have to stay away from school? How long for?

Did you miss school? Did you miss your friends? Did

the doctor come to see you? What was the matter with you? What did he give you to make you feel better?

Is there anything that you like about feeling ill?

If you had flu like Hamid, what should you do to help yourself get better?

If Mum or Dad are ill, do you help them? What can you do to help them feel better?

Have you ever missed anything special because you were ill? What was it? How did you feel?

William and the Pied Piper (More Robins)

General discussion

The story

Did you enjoy this story? What did you like about it?

What went wrong for William during the play? How did it happen?

How did the boys know that they weren't in the school hall anymore?

What was making the scuffling and rustling sound in the corners of the shop?

How did they know that they were in a time long ago?

Look at the picture on page 21. There is something there that doesn't belong if the story took place a long time ago. What is it?

What do you think of the mayor for giving the Piper just one coin?

The Pied Piper story

Do you know where Hamelin is?

Do you think it is a true story? Why? Why not?

How is the ending of 'William and the Piper' different from the real story of 'The Pied Piper'?

Which ending do you prefer? Why?

Some stories have a moral to them – that is something that we should learn from them. What do you think the moral of this story would be?

Do you think that the Piper was right to lead the children away? Why? Why not?

In the real story, the only child who doesn't go into the cave is a little boy with a bad leg (like Hamid). How do you think his parents felt when he was the only child left in Hamelin?

Going to the theatre

Have you ever been to a theatre? What did you see? What is it like inside?

What sort of things are performed in a theatre?

Many theatres have rows of seats at different heights. The bottom level is called the stalls. The middle level is called the circle. The upper level is called the upper circle. (They are called circles because they are often in a circular shape.)

Where would you like to sit for a show? Why?

Halfway through the show, there is a break called an interval. You can buy drinks or ice creams during the interval. Have you ever been to the theatre and had a drink or ice cream in the interval? What did you buy?

Lots of people are needed to work in a theatre to put on a show. Can you think of some of the jobs that they might do?

If you worked in a theatre, what job would you like to do? Why?

Stage 10

The holiday (*Robins*)

Discussion pointers

Page 1
Why do you think Wilf and Wilma have made a journey on an aeroplane?
Where do you think they have come from, and why have they come by aeroplane?
How can you tell that the airport is only a small one?

Pages 2/3
Why do you think Wilf and Wilma haven't visited their grandparents before?
Where do your grandparents live? Do you visit them? How do you get there?
Why haven't Wilf and Wilma's parents come with them?
Have you ever been to stay with anyone without your parents being with you? What was it like?
Why does Wilf think the sun is hot? Is the sun hot all the time where his grandparents live?

Pages 4/5
Why would it be nice to live on an island like Wilf and Wilma's grandparents?
Why does Grandfather have a boat?
Why would you like to live somewhere where the sun is always hot and the sea is warm and blue?

Pages 6/7
Why did Wilma think her grandparents had a fantastic place to live?
Would you like to live near a beach? Why?

Pages 8/9
What sort of boat does Grandfather own?
Why had Grandfather taken his boat out of the water?
Why did Wilma offer to help Grandfather paint the boat?

Page 10
Do you remember the story when Wilf helped to paint the tree house? Do you remember what happened in that story?★
★ *The storm* (Stage 4)

Page 11
Why do you think Wilma wants to visit the little islands so badly?
Why can't they go straightaway?

Page 12
Why did Wilf and Wilma enjoy swimming in the sea?
Why do you think the sea is so warm in the Caribbean?

Page 13
Why is it fun to swim with masks and flippers? What is the breathing tube called?
What are cousins? Do you have any cousins? Are they older or younger than you?

Pages 14/15
What is the giant fish called?
Why is the ray such a wide, flat shape?
Why did Wilma wish she had a camera?
Why would you like to swim in a lovely place like this?

Pages 16/17
Why are Wilf and Wilma's cousins trying on costumes?
What is a carnival?
Would you like to dress up and go to a carnival? What would you go as?

Pages 18/19
What was the giant spool once used for?
What did Wilf have to do to make the giant spool roll forward?
Why didn't Grandfather dress up?

Pages 20/21
What sort of band is playing on the back of the lorry?
What does a steel band sound like?
Which costume do you like best of all?
Why does one of the men look so tall?

Page 22
What is a coconut?
Where do coconuts grow? Why don't coconuts grow in Britain?
Look through the book and point to a tree on which coconuts grow.

Page 23
What is unusual about the rain that falls in the Caribbean?

Page 24
Why do you think Grandfather was worried?
What is a weather forecast?

Page 25
Why did Grandfather put wooden shutters up at the windows? What does it tell you about the sort of storms that sometimes blow in the Caribbean?
Why do you think there isn't any glass in the windows of the house?

Pages 26/27
How can you see that it is a very bad storm indeed?
What is a very strong wind called?
Why were Wilf and Wilma frightened by the storm?
What will happen if the storm becomes much worse?
What is the name of the very worst kind of storm in the Caribbean?

Pages 28/29
What sort of damage had the storm done?
What did Grandmother think was a good job?
How do you think the boat had got on to the beach?
Why did Grandfather think he had been lucky?

Pages 30/31
What would it be like to spend an afternoon on a boat like this one?
Why do you think there is a little ladder going into the water?
Why do you think Grandfather's seat is so high up above that water?
How do you know the boat is not moving in the picture? Why do you think the boat has stopped?
What do you think Wilf and Grandfather are looking at?

Page 32
Why do you suppose Wilf and Wilma felt both sorry and glad that the holiday was over?
What do you think would be the first thing they would tell Biff and Chip?

Which part of their holiday do you think Wilf and Wilma would remember the most?

Going on holiday
Would you like to spend a holiday on a Caribbean island? How would you get there?
What do you like to do most? How is a holiday by the sea in this country different from a holiday in the Caribbean?
Why did Wilf and Wilma swim with the masks and flippers?
Would you enjoy doing something like that on holiday? Why?
What sort of holiday would you like to have most of all?

Grandparents
What do you call your grandparents? Do you have different names for all of them?
Which grandparents do you see, or visit, the most? Why? Can you say how many grandchildren both sets of your grandparents have?
What is special about any of your grandparents?

Staying away from home
In the story, how do you know it was the first time that Wilf and Wilma had stayed with their grandparents on the island? Do you think Wilf and Wilma were homesick? Have you ever been homesick? What is it like to be upset when you are away from home? How brave do you think you can be when you are away from home?

The storm
How was the storm on the island different from storms that you have known?
Have you ever seen really heavy rain? What was it like?
What happens to the drains and gutters when there is really heavy rain?
What happens to the trees when there is really strong wind?
What words describe bad storms and strong wind?

General discussion

The story
What did you learn about the Caribbean from this story? Where is the Caribbean?

The secret plans (*Robins*)

Discussion pointers

Page 1
What is an office? What sort of work do people do in offices?
Why do Anneena's mum and dad have to clean the carpets in the evenings rather than during the day?
Why do you think that they have to take Anneena with them sometimes?
Have you ever been to the place where your mum or dad work? What was it like?

Pages 2/3
Why do you think Anneena got bored sitting in an office? What would she rather be doing?
What do people keep in filing cabinets?
Why was the man's office in such a mess?
What do people mean by a 'spring-clean'?

Pages 4/5
Why didn't the man want to keep all the papers on the floor?
Why did Anneena want the big pieces of paper?

Pages 6/7
Why did Anneena take the paper to school?
Why are schools always glad to have scrap paper?
Why did Mr Johnson cut the paper up?
What is a secret? What is 'top secret'? Why are top secret papers and plans important?

Pages 8/9
Why did Mr Johnson say the last zoo trip was spoiled by rain? What happened? Do you remember the story?*
What did Chip ask Mr Johnson? Why is it hard not to eat your packed lunch before it's lunchtime?
What happened to Biff's packed lunch?
Which animal would you like to study if you went to a zoo?
* See *The outing, Owls*

Page 10
What has the man lost?
What has happened to the secret plans?

What might happen to the man if he can't find them?
Have you ever lost anything important?

Page 11
Why was the man in trouble?
Why do people go red? What is a word which means 'to go red'?
What do you think the Prime Minister said to the man when he told her he had lost the papers?

Page 12
Why wouldn't you like to be the man at that moment?
What does it feel like to be in trouble?
What will have to be done about the lost papers?

Page 13
Why was Anneena's mum worried?
Who do you think the people were?

Page 14
Why was Kipper pleased with himself?
Have you ever done a piece of work that you've been really pleased with? What was it?

Page 15
Who were the visitors to the school?
How would you feel if you were one of the children in the class?
Where will the visitors have to go next?
Why do you think they might have problems in getting all the paper back from the children at the zoo?

Pages 16/17
What do you know about tigers? Where do wild tigers live?
Why are tigers dangerous animals?
Do you think they mind being in a zoo? Why?
What did Chip hope was a joke? Was it?

Pages 18/19
Why was Mr Johnson worried? Why do you think he might have got into trouble too?
Why do you think the children were worried when they heard what had happened?

Pages 20/21
Why did the children have to go back to school early?
Why is there a police car in front of the coach? Why does the man on the motorway bridge look surprised?

Pages 22/23

Why was it important to check that every bit of paper had been found?

Pages 24/25

Why were the children better than the grown-ups at putting the plans back together?
Where do you think the two missing pieces of paper are?

Page 26

Why did Chip think he would be in trouble?
What do you think Mr Johnson said when he saw Chip's drawing?

Page 27

Why didn't Anneena want to say where the other piece of paper was?
Why is it better to own up when you've done something wrong?

Page 28

Why were the grown-ups pleased? Why were the children fed up?

Pages 30/31

What is going on in this picture?
How can you tell that one of the children doesn't like pizza? What is a pizza?
What would you like to eat on a picnic?

Page 32

If that is the man who gave Anneena the paper, why do you think he is working in the zoo, now?

General discussion

The story

Whom did you feel sorry for in the story?
I felt sorry for a) the children in Mr Johnson's class,
b) Kipper, c) Anneena's mum, d) Mr Johnson,
e) Anneena, f) Chip, because ...
Were some of the people in the story foolish? Did they make mistakes? How about a) the man, b) Mr Johnson, c) Anneena and Chip?
Did any parts of the story make you laugh? Which bits did you think were funniest?

Plans

What are plans? Why do people use them? Do you ever need a plan to make a construction kit toy or a Lego model?
Do your mum or dad ever use plans in the home? What sort of plans are needed for cooking, dressmaking, putting something together?
Why does a builder need a plan? What might a house look like if it did not have a plan to tell the builder what to do?

Secrets

Why do important grown-ups, like the Prime Minister, have secrets?
What is a secret? Have you ever had a secret of your own? Have you ever had to keep one of someone else's? Why is it important never to give away a secret? Why is it important for your friends to trust you?

Ghost tricks (More Robins)

General discussion

The story

Did you enjoy the story? What was your favourite part? Why?
Did you think that Ann and Jess's plan would work? Why?
What sort of man is Mr Smart? How would you describe him?
Did the villagers want another supermarket? Why not?
Do you think that Horton looked like a beautiful village? Would you like to live there? Why? Why not?
How different would living in a village be, do you think, from living in a town? Which would you prefer? Why didn't Ann and Jess feel scared when they first met the ghost boy?

Times long ago

Look at the picture on pages 8 and 9. There are lots of things that are different from a modern day room. What can you see that you wouldn't see in your living room or lounge at home? What sort of lights do you think they might have had?
Are there any radiators? How did they keep warm?
What have you got in your living room or lounge that you can't see here? (Many of these things use electricity.

The ghost boy lived about three hundred and fifty years ago when electricity was not invented.)

What can you see on pages 10 and 11? These are servants who are paid to cook for the owners of the house. What types of food are being cooked? Do we eat some of these foods today? What is cooking on the fire? What have you got in your kitchen that they don't have here? (Are they also things that need electricity to work?)

Look carefully – can you see a sink? Where do you think they might do the washing up?

Would you like to eat this meal? What would you like to eat most?

Look at the picture on pages 16 and 17. How are the people's clothes different from those we wear today? Does their hair look different? How? Do you think their clothes look comfortable? Why? Why not? Would you like to wear these clothes?

How are they spending their time? What activities are they doing?

Museums

What is a museum? Have you ever been to a museum? What sort of museum was it? Did you enjoy it? There are museums now that have special rooms, especially if they are science museums, where children are allowed to touch things and in some cases do experiments. Have you ever been to a museum like that? Where was it and what did you enjoy doing? Why would it be good for the people of Horton to have their own local museum? What sort of things do you think they might put in that museum?

The discovery (More Robins)

General discussion

The story

Did you enjoy this story? Why? Why not?

Did you feel sorry for Amy when she thought that she was going to have to leave her home?

Would you like to live in the country? Why? Why not?

Why is a Land Rover usually a good type of car to have if you live in the country?

Look at the sorts of clothes that Amy and her parents wear. Why are they suitable for living in the country and for working in the rain?

What is Mrs Long's job? What does an archaeologist do? Do you think it is an interesting job? Would you like to do it?

Mrs Long was thrilled with the discovery. How long did she say that she had been looking for the villa?

What had archaeologists found in the area before this big discovery?

On the day of the big discovery who came to the village? Why?

What difference would this discovery make to Amy and her parents?

What do you think would happen to all the coins and jars that they had found?

Do you think that all the villagers would be happy now that their village was famous?

What difference would it make to the village?

Caravan holidays

This story takes place in Wales. Have you ever been to Wales? Can you remember where you stayed?

Have you ever stayed in a caravan? What was it like? Did you like it?

What exactly is a caravan? Some are mobile (you can tow them behind a car). Some are static (a big lorry drives them to one place and they stay there).

What do you like best about staying in a caravan?

What don't you like about staying in a caravan?

Have you ever been in a caravan when it rains? What does it sound like?

When you have a big family in a caravan when it rains for a long time it can be very difficult. Why?

What do you do to keep yourself busy when it rains?

Archaeologists

Why do you think the work that archaeologists do is so important?

Archaeologists have to work very carefully and very slowly. They usually use brushes to brush away the soil. Why? What could have happened to the vase when Amy's mum and Mrs Long tried to pull it out?

Most vases or jars (they are called pottery) are not found in one piece. They are often broken and the archaeologist works hard to put them together again. It is rather like doing a jigsaw puzzle. Do you like doing jigsaw puzzles? Do you think that being an archaeologist is rather a dirty job? Why?

Where do all the things that archaeologists find go?

Have you been to a museum and seen some very old things like Amy found? What did you see?

Robins and More Robins language activities grid

	COMPREHENSION	SEQUENCING	CLOZE	IMAGINATIVE WRITING	NON-FICTION WRITING	EXTRACTING INFORMATION	ALPHABETICAL ORDER	GRAMMAR	PUNCTUATION
Stage 6									
The Dump	p 65	p 67	p 67	p 66					
Max makes breakfast	p 68	p 70	p 70	p 69					
Stage 7									
The old vase	p 71			p 72		p 73			
William and the dog	p 74		p 76	p 75			p 76		
The long journey	p 77			p 78		p 79			
Mum's new car	p 80		p 82	p 81			p 82		
Stage 8									
The emergency	p 83	p 85		p 84					
Kate and the sheep	p 86				p 87			p 88	
The surprise	p 89	p 91		p 90					
William's mistake	p 92			p 93				p 94	
Stage 9									
The photograph	p 95		p 97		p 96				p 97
The village show	p 98	p 100		p 99					
A proper bike	p 101			p 102					p 103
Treasure hunt	p 104			p 105	p 106				
Hamid does his best	p 107	p 109		p 108					
William and the Pied Piper	p 110			p 111		p 112			
Stage 10									
The holiday	p 113			p 114	p 115				
The secret plans	p 116		p 118	p 117				p 118	
Ghost tricks	p 119		p 121	p 120				p 121	
The discovery	p 122			p 123					p 124

Thinking about the story

Using pages 1–5 of the story

1   *The Dump* is a story about

☐   treasure in a rubbish dump   ☐   a children's playground

☐   a lost dog   ☐   a bike ride

2   What is the name of the boy who tells the story?

☐   Sam   ☐   Ben

☐   Mike   ☐   Lenny

3   At The Dump there was somewhere for them to

☐   swim   ☐   buy an ice-cream

☐   ride their bikes   ☐   go shopping

4   What could they play with at The Dump?

☐   toys and games   ☐   sand and shells

☐   old tyres and bits of wood   ☐   swings and a slide

5   Why did the wall look a mess?

☐   They hadn't got any paint.   ☐   The children had a fight.

☐   The paint spilt.   ☐   They all had different ideas.

6   Why was The Dump a good place to play?

☐   It had swings and slides.

☐   It was a safe place to play and had everything they wanted.

☐   It was a long way from where they lived.

Writing a letter

Think about a playground where you like to play. How would you feel if workmen came to build houses or a new road there? Write a letter to the local council giving at least three reasons why you think the playground should stay.

_____   write your address here

_____

_____

_____   write the date here

Dear Sir,

_____

_____

_____

_____

_____

_____

Yours faithfully,

_____   your name

Filling in gaps

Read the words in the passage and then try to fill in the gaps with the word that you think fits best. The words in the boxes will help you.

I looked over the fence.

I saw my ball, _____ I saw something else.

Two men were loading things _____ to a lorry.

I didn't want the men to _____ me, so I jumped down quickly.

'There's something funny _____ on,' I said.

'Two men are loading up a _____.'

'I bet they're stealing things,' said Tracey.

'Get the _____ of the lorry but mind they don't see you.'

_____ told my brother about the two men.

'I'm sure _____ were stealing,' I said.

lorry	on	they	going
I	number	see	but

Putting in order

Here are some events in the story. Put them in the right order by numbering each box. The first one is done for you.

☐ Lenny saw some men stealing.

[1] The children liked to play in The Dump.

☐ The Council gave the children a new playground.

☐ Some workmen came to clean up The Dump.

☐ The Council gave the children a new Dump to play in.

Thinking about the story

Using pages 1–5 of the story

1   *Max makes breakfast* is a story about

☐   Max's birthday   ☐   Grandad's birthday

☐   Kerry's birthday   ☐   Mum's birthday

2   Who is wrapping a present?

☐   Max   ☐   Kerry

☐   Mum   ☐   Dad

3   What did Kerry want to make for Grandad's birthday?

☐   a card   ☐   a cake

☐   a present   ☐   a hat

4   Where did Kerry decide to do her painting?

☐   on her bed   ☐   on the bedroom table

☐   on the kitchen table   ☐   on the kitchen floor

5   Why couldn't Kerry paint Max's swimming trunks green?

☐   She didn't have the right sort of blue.

☐   She didn't have the right sort of green.

☐   She didn't have any green.

☐   She didn't have any blue.

6   Who groaned 'Oh no! Is that the time?'

☐   Mum   ☐   Dad

☐   Kerry   ☐   Grandad

Writing a recipe

Max made a special breakfast for Bubbles. Wanda the Witch is making a special cake for her friend's birthday, but she put some very strange things in it. Can you write out the recipe for her?

The different things that you put in the cake are called the ingredients, for example, 12 fried ants. What you have to do to make it is called the method.

Wanda's special birthday cake

Ingredients

Method

```
1


2


3


4


5
```

Filling in gaps

Read the words in the passage and then try to fill in the gaps with the word that you think fits best. The words in the boxes will help you.

Max went into Mum and Dad's room to look _____ himself in the mirror.

There were all sorts of _____ things on Mum's dressing table.

This gave Max an _____.

He decided to make another breakfast for Bubbles.

First _____ got some white powder and poured it on to _____ pillow.

Then he found some cream and added that.

_____ he poured perfume into the mixture.

When Max had _____ making breakfast for Bubbles he sat his teddy

on _____ bed.

| idea | the | a | at |
| exciting | Then | he | finished |

Putting in order

Here are some events in the story. Put them in the right order by numbering each box. The first one is done for you.

[ ] Max made a mess in the bedroom.

[ ] Max made a mess in the kitchen.

[ ] Grandad helped them to clean up the mess.

[1] Kerry painted a card for Grandad.

[ ] Kerry and Max began to cry.

Thinking about the story

Using pages 12–16 of the story

1   The story is about

☐   an old clock   ☐   an old vase

☐   an old plate   ☐   an old chair

2   Who carried the vase to the antique shop?

☐   Lenny   ☐   Ann

☐   Mel   ☐   Tracey

3   Who did they see on the way to the antique shop?

☐   Lenny Brown   ☐   Mrs Ramage

☐   Ann Godfrey   ☐   Mr Gohil

4   How did Ann Godfrey describe the vase?

She said it was

☐   old   ☐   horrible

☐   special   ☐   beautiful

5   What did Mel do when Ann grabbed the vase?

☐   He ran away.   ☐   He began to cry.

☐   He screamed.   ☐   He shut his eyes.

6   Why did Tracey feel very, very angry?

She was angry because

☐   the vase was broken.

☐   Ann Godfrey had lost the vase.

☐   Ann Godfrey called Mel a 'cry baby'.

☐   the vase was lost.

Writing a story

Imagine that you bought a vase from an antique shop like the one in the story *The old vase*. You gave it to your grandma for her birthday. What happened next? Tell the story.

_____

_____

_____

_____

_____

_____

_____

Finding information

Summer Fair

at

Peckworth School

Saturday 23rd June

at 2 o'clock

lucky dip	ice-creams	candy floss
tombola	splash the teacher	bouncy castle
toy stall	donkey rides	coconut shy

ADULTS – 40p   CHILDREN – 20p

1   Where is the fair going to be held?

☐   Greenwood School   ☐   Peckworth School

☐   Peckworth House   ☐   Peckindale School

2   What time does the fair start?

☐   2 o'clock   ☐   3 o'clock

☐   4 o'clock   ☐   1 o'clock

3   What is the date of the fair?

The fair is on _____.

4   How much does it cost children to go to the fair?

It costs _____.

5   Which stalls would you like to have a go on? Why?

_____

Thinking about the story

Using pages 12–16 of the story

coffee	Shopping Centre	Green Park
chair	A waiter	poodle

1   Where was the cafe?

The cafe was in the _____.

2   What did William tie Toffee's lead to?

William tied Toffee's lead to a _____.

3   What were the man and woman at the next table drinking?

The man and woman were drinking _____.

4   What type of dog did the woman have?

The woman had a _____.

5   Who yelled 'Get that dog out of here!'?

_____ yelled 'Get that dog out of here!'

6   Where did Hamid say that they should go next?

Hamid said that they should go to _____.

Finishing a story

Finish this story.

It was a quiet, peaceful day. The sun was shining. Mum was busy painting the window frames and next door Mrs Jones was hanging out her washing. Suddenly, our dog Sam saw Mrs Jones's cat and snarled ...

_____

_____

_____

_____

_____

_____

_____

Filling in gaps

Read the words in the passage and then try to fill in the gaps with the word that you think fits best. The words in the boxes will help you.

Suddenly Toffee was off again.

He ran straight into _____ big department store.

'Not again,' gasped William.

The shop _____ all sorts of food.

William and Hamid ran through _____ doors.

Everybody was trying to catch Toffee.

People were _____ over each other and displays of food were

crashing _____.

'Get that dog out of here!' yelled the manager.

_____ went straight on to the meat department.

Toffee saw _____ he wanted.

He jumped on to one of the _____ and grabbed a big fish.

| counters | sold | down | the |
| Toffee | what | falling | a |

Using the alphabet

Tick the word which comes **first** in the dictionary.

☐ lead
☐ park
☐ dog
☐ walk

Tick the word which comes **last** in the dictionary.

☐ train
☐ station
☐ platform
☐ inspector

Thinking about the story

Using pages 1–5 of the story

1   The long journey is a story about

☐   a long coach journey   ☐   a long train journey

☐   a long bus journey   ☐   a long car journey

2   When Kerry woke up she felt

☐   worried   ☐   sad

☐   excited   ☐   scared

3   What was Dad packing in the cardboard box?

☐   clothes   ☐   food

☐   toys   ☐   books

4   Why did Dad want to leave early?

☐   He wanted to go to the shops.

☐   He wanted to get some petrol.

☐   There was going to be a lot of traffic.

☐   The car wouldn't start.

5   What did Kerry have for her breakfast?

☐   toast   ☐   a choc-ice

☐   an egg   ☐   an apple

6   Why wasn't Grandad going with them on holiday?

☐   He hadn't got a car.

☐   There was no room.

☐   He wanted some peace and quiet.

☐   He was going on another holiday.

Going on holiday

You are going on holiday to the seaside by coach. What do you think you would take with you?

Fill this suitcase with all the things that you would like to take with you.

Describe your journey. Was it a long one?

Was there a lot of traffic? How did you feel when you first saw the sea? Did anything go wrong?

_____

_____

_____

_____

_____

_____

_____

Finding information

Holiday cottage

- good sea views
- close to the sea
- 3 bedrooms
- garden with swing
- shops nearby
- good for children
- no dogs
- washing machine

Book now!

You could come in June or July.

Telephone 01643 4321

This is an advert for a holiday cottage. Read it carefully and then answer these questions.

1   Where is the cottage?

☐   by a river   ☐   close to a town

☐   in the country   ☐   close to the sea

2   How many bedrooms has the cottage got?

☐   1 bedroom   ☐   2 bedrooms

☐   3 bedrooms   ☐   4 bedrooms

3   Could you take your dog there?

_____

4   When could you stay in this cottage?

_____

5   What do you think it means by 'good sea views'?

_____

6   Would you like to stay in this cottage? Why? Why not?

_____

_____

Thinking about the story

Using pages 12–15 of the story

multi-storey	wedding cake	old
car park attendants	Aunt Vicky's	suspicious

1   Who's wedding were they going to?

They were going to _____ wedding.

2   Which car did Lisa like best?

Lisa liked the _____ car best.

3   On the morning of the wedding, what did they have to collect from the town?

They had to collect the _____ from the town.

4   What sort of car park did Mum park the car in?

Mum parked the car in a _____ car park.

5   What did Lisa think of the man hiding behind the pillar?

Lisa thought the man looked _____.

6   Who did Mum say would keep an eye on things in the car park?

Mum said that the _____

would keep an eye on things.

Writing a story

You are the owner of a very big smart car and you have your own chauffeur. (A chauffeur is someone who drives people where they want to go.) Where would you ask him to take you? Would you take some friends or family with you? Write about your day.

_____

_____

_____

_____

_____

_____

_____

_____

_____

_____

_____

_____

Filling in gaps

Read the words in the passage and then try to fill in the gaps with the word that you think fits best. The words in the boxes will help you.

There were cars of all shapes, sizes and colours.

_____ of them were too expensive.

Some of them were _____ bangers.

'I can't seem to make up my mind,' _____ Mum.

Then Mum saw it.

'That's it!' she said. '_____ the car I'm going to buy. It's just what _____ been looking for.'

'But it hasn't got a roof,' _____ Lisa.

'Yes it has,' said Mum. 'It has a _____ roof.'

Mum was very excited about the new car.

_____ went into the showroom and bought it straight away.

folding	That's	said	She
said	Some	I've	old

Using the alphabet

Tick the word which comes **first** in the dictionary.

- [ ] new
- [ ] car
- [ ] showroom
- [ ] old

Tick the word which comes **last** in the dictionary.

- [ ] cake
- [ ] wedding
- [ ] ribbon
- [ ] church

Thinking about the story

Using pages 3–7 of the story

Mrs Knight	on the floor
kitchen	William

1   Who shouted through the letter box?

_____ shouted through the letter box.

2   Which window did they look through?

They looked through the _____ window.

3   Where was Mrs Lacey lying?

Mrs Lacey was lying _____.

4   Who had a spare key?

_____ had a spare key.

5   What did Mrs Knight tell William and Hamid to do?

Mrs Knight told William and Hamid to _____

_____.

6   Where was the nearest phone box?

The nearest phone box was _____

_____.

Writing a story

These pictures tell a story. It is about a child trying to help a cat stuck up in a tree. Tell the story in your own words.

_____

_____

_____

_____

_____

_____

_____

Putting in order

What would you do if someone you knew had an accident? Look at these sentences. Put them in the right order by numbering each box.

- [ ] Say who you are and where you are.
- [ ] Find a telephone.
- [ ] Say if you want police, ambulance or fire.
- [ ] Ring 999.
- [ ] Tell them what has happened.

Write the sentences in the correct order on the lines below.

1 _____

2 _____

3 _____

4 _____

5 _____

Thinking about the story

Using pages 26–29 of the story

| blanket | Mr Munday |

| cardboard box | too busy |

1   What was the name of the farmer in the story?

The farmer was called _____.

2   Why couldn't Mr Munday look after the baby lambs?

Mr Munday couldn't look after the baby lambs because he was _____.

3   What did they wrap the lamb in?

They wrapped the lamb in a _____.

4   What did Mum put the lamb in when they got home?

Mum put the lamb in a _____.

5   Why did they put the cardboard box by the stove?

They put the cardboard box by the stove _____

_____.

6   What did Mum say that Kate and Jo had to do for the lamb?

Mum said that Kate and Jo had to _____

_____.

Write a country code

What is happening in the pictures? What rule are the people breaking? What other rules should people keep when they are in the country?

Write four rules to make your own country code.

My Country Code

by

_____

1 _____

2 _____

3 _____

4 _____

Joining sentences

These sentences can be joined together. There are special words which do this. Choose the word that you think fits best for each pair of sentences and put it in the right space. The first one is done for you.

so	but	and
and	when	but

1   'We can't take him for walks **and** he won't fetch sticks.'   (page 1)

2   They waited and waited _____ Mr Munday didn't come.   (page 12)

3   They went to the big field _____ climbed on the gate.   (page 11)

4   'I'm far too busy to look after baby lambs _____ I'd like you to look after it.'

(page 27)

5   The old ewe slowed down _____ she saw Mr Mudge.   (page 20)

6   'You were only trying to help me _____ you must never open gates when there are animals in a field.'   (page 24)

Thinking about the story

Using pages 10–13 of the story

| litter tray | Lucky |
| too young | both |

1 Which kitten did Dad decide to take home?

Dad decided to take _____ kittens home.

2 On the way home, Dad bought the kittens a basket to sleep in, a rubber mouse and what else?

On the way home, Dad bought the kittens a basket to sleep in, a rubber mouse and a _____.

3 What did Ben call his kitten?

Ben called his kitten _____.

4 Why couldn't the kittens go outside?

The kittens couldn't go outside because they were _____.

5 What did Ben and Laura have to do for the kittens every day?

Every day Ben and Laura had to _____

_____.

6 How did Laura describe the kittens?

Laura said _____

_____.

Writing a story

Look at these pictures. They tell a story about some children who are given a pet.
What happens? Tell the story.

_____

_____

_____

_____

_____

_____

_____

Putting in order

Here are some of the events in the story. Read them carefully.

Put them in the correct order by numbering the boxes and then write them out below. The first one is done for you.

☐ 'Come in, come in! I've been expecting you,' she said. 'There are just two left.'

1 'Get in the car,' said Dad. 'It's a surprise.'

☐ Dad carried Ben up the stairs.

☐ A lady came to the door.

☐ They drove to some flats on the other side of the town.

☐ Dad rang the bell at one of the flats.

1   'Get in the car,' said Dad. 'It's a surprise.'

2   _____

     _____

3   _____

     _____

4   _____

     _____

5   _____

     _____

6   _____

     _____

Thinking about the story

Using pages 13–15 of the story

climbing	old wooden shed
oak	brave but nervous

1   What sort of tree had Toffee stopped at the foot of?

Toffee had stopped at the foot of an _____ tree.

2   What did William think he was quite good at?

William thought that he was quite good at _____.

3   How did William feel when he climbed the tree?

William felt _____.

4   What could William see in the distance?

In the distance William could see an _____.

5   William could see two men getting out of a car. What sort of car was it?

William saw two men getting out of a _____

_____.

6   What were the men doing to another man?

The two men were _____

_____.

Writing a story

Look at these pictures. They tell a story.

You are a boy like the one in the pictures. Write a story about your school sports day.
Remember to describe how you felt.

_____

_____

_____

_____

_____

_____

_____

Joining sentences

Look at these sentences carefully. They can be joined together by putting words in the middle. Choose the word which you think fits best and put it in the right space. The first one is done for you.

but	when	and

and	or	but

1   'Well I must have my tea now, **and** you should never go swimming after eating,'
      said William.   (page 7)

2   It wasn't easy to climb the tree _____ William managed it in the end.

                                                                                  (page 14)

3   William was miserable _____ he thought of the things that Tom and Emma
      had said.   (page 12)

4   'I've been running races all day _____ now I've got to take this dog for a walk,'
      moaned William.   (page 10)

5   'Hold on to his lead, then, _____ you'll never keep up with him,' shouted Tom.

                                                                                  (page 11)

6   It wasn't very high _____ William had a good view from there.   (page 14)

Thinking about the story

Using pages 16–19 of the story

1   What was William doing on Saturday morning?

On Saturday morning William was _____

_____ .

2   Who said that they would help William with his project?

_____ said that she would help William with his project.

3   Where had his sister been?

_____

_____

4   His sister found a book with a very old photograph in it. What was the photograph of?

_____

_____

5   What was different about the outside of the school?

_____

_____

6   What did William notice that he had in his classroom now but they didn't have in
     the photograph?

_____

_____

_____

Writing a diary

A diary is a book in which someone writes down what happens each day.

Write a diary for a day at school.

My diary for _____	date
morning	
_____	What time did you get up?
_____	What lessons did you do?
afternoon	
_____	What did you have for lunch?
_____	Who did you play with?
evening	
_____	What did you have for tea?
_____	What time did you go to bed?

Which part of the day didn't you like?

_____

Which part of the day did you like best?

_____

Filling in gaps

Read the words in the passage and then try to fill in the gaps with the words which you think fit best.

William didn't know what to do.

He was too _____ to say anything.

He watched the other children dip _____ pens into the ink-wells and start to write.

'_____ have to try and do what they do,' he _____.

There was not a sound in the classroom except _____ scratching of the pens.

William did his best to _____ with his ink pen.

But it wasn't easy.

He _____ lots of blots.

'Stop writing!' snapped the teacher. 'Put _____ your pens and stand up quietly.'

Using question marks

When someone asks a question we put a question mark | ? | at the end of the sentence.
Put a | ? | by the sentences below that ask questions. Put a full stop at the end of the
other sentences.

1   Why can't ducks fly upside down

2   What was it like in the old days

3   William looked at the old photograph

4   Why not write about your school in the old days

5   On Saturday morning William was watching cartoons

6   Will you help me

Thinking about the story

Using pages 2–5 of the story

1   How often was the village show held?

The village show was held _____.

2   What did people grow for the village show?

People grew _____ and _____ for the village show.

3   What did people make for the village show?

_____

_____

4   What was Dad entering for the village show?

_____

_____

5   Who always won the prize for the best wine?

_____

_____

6   Why did Kate want to make dandelion wine?

_____

_____

Writing a story

FIRST PRIZE

awarded to

....

for
the tallest beanstalk

1st

Write a story about winning first prize for the tallest beanstalk. Where did you get the bean seeds? Were they magic? Where did you plant them? What did the plant look like when it started growing? In what kind of show did you enter the plant? How did you get it there? What did people say?

Putting in order

Here are some events in the story. Write out the sentences in the correct order. The first one is done for you.

They put all the flowers in a big pan.

Kate and Jo wanted to make some dandelion wine.

At the end, Kate added some yellow paint.

They tipped in sugar and wine gums.

The girls picked lots and lots of dandelions.

The girls filled the pan with cold water.

1   Kate and Jo wanted to make some dandelion wine.

2   _____

_____

3   _____

_____

4   _____

_____

5   _____

_____

6   _____

_____

Thinking about the story

Using pages 16–19 of the story

1   Who put the bikes in the trailer?

_____ put the bikes in the trailer.

2   Where did he put Anneena's bike?

He put Anneena's bike_____.

3   Where were they going for their bike ride?

_____

4   How do you think Anneena felt when Chip said 'We can't go too far if Anneena has to ride that old bike.'?

_____

_____

5   Where had Wilma's mum put all the picnic things?

_____

_____

6   Why did Wilma's mum not want Anneena to carry all the picnic things in her carrier?

_____

_____

Writing a story

Write a story about a bike which flies. Think about how you got the bike. Was it a present? Did someone give it to you? How did you find out it could fly? What makes it fly? Where have you been on your bike?

_____

_____

_____

_____

_____

_____

Using full stops and capital letters

Anneena wrote this letter to her grandfather thanking him for her 'proper' bike. She told him all about the bike ride too, but she forgot to put in all the full stops and capital letters. Will you do this for her? Read the letter carefully and then put the full stops and capital letters where you think they should go. You could use a red crayon. We have done the first few for you.

Remember that you need a capital letter for the beginning of a sentence and for the name of a person or a place.

---

21 Fincham Road

Dagworth

Sunday 24th June

Dear Grandfather,

thank you very much for the bike i went for a bike ride and a picnic with wilf and wilma we went to kingswood forest it was really good wilma's dad took us in the car he put my bike on the roof rack we went for a long bike ride and then had a picnic by the lake i put everyone's bags in my carrier after the picnic, we paddled in the water and climbed a tree on the way back wilma fell off her bike she hurt her leg so wilma's mum rode my bike and wilma sat in the carrier i think that my bike is the best bike in the whole world

thank you grandfather

with love from

anneena

Thinking about the story

Using pages 16–21 of the story

1   Who was following William and Hamid into the maze?

_____ and _____ were following William and

Hamid into the maze.

2   Where did they find the second envelope?

The second envelope was _____

_____.

3   What was on the back of the envelope?

_____

_____

4   William and Hamid stumbled over a big bundle. What was inside the bundle?

_____

_____

5   Why did the imposter want to steal the big balloon as well as the paintings?

_____

_____

6   How do you think William and Hamid felt when Toby and Jim took their prize paper?

_____

_____

Writing a story

Toffee is up to his tricks again! When he chases the cat, he knocks down the sandbags. The sandbags help to hold the balloon down. Hamid and William are stuck in the balloon as it goes higher and higher into the sky. What do you think happens next? Write the story.

_____

_____

_____

_____

_____

_____

_____

_____

_____

Writing instructions

Hamid is lost in the maze. Tell William where he has to go to find Hamid.

You will need to use these instructions:

turn left

turn right

go straight on

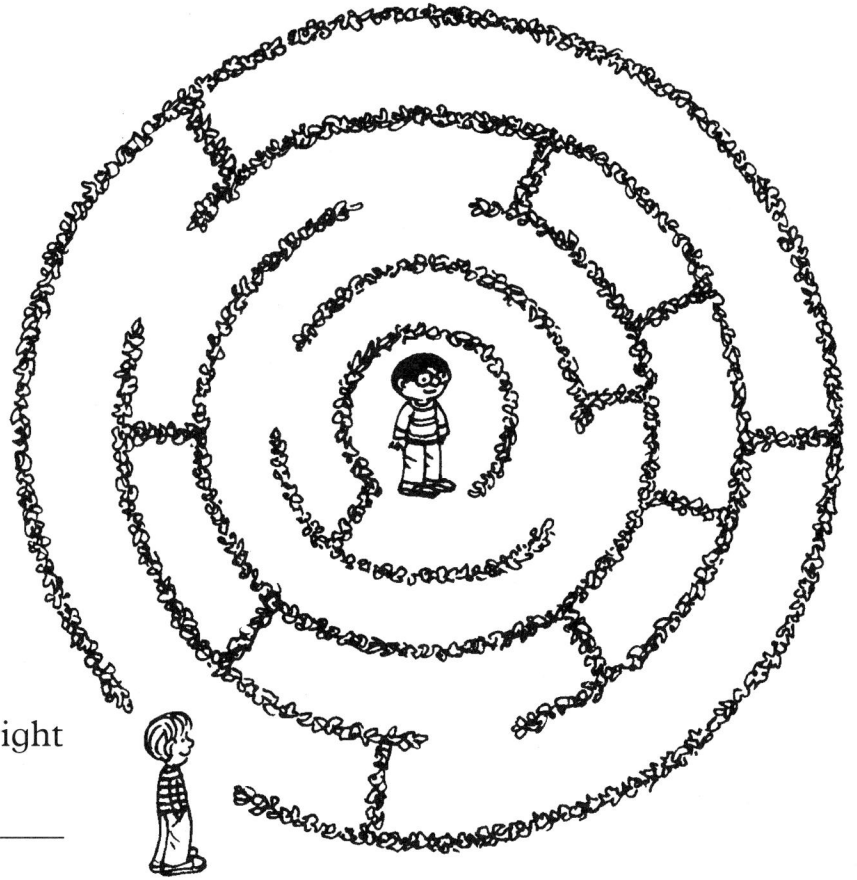

remember   left ←——————→ right

1 _____

2 _____

3 _____

4 _____

5 _____

6 _____

7 _____

8 _____

Thinking about the story

Using pages 22–25 of the story

1   Why did Mrs Patel think they should cancel the match?

Mrs Patel thought they should cancel the match because _____

_____.

2   Who shouted 'Hamid is our best player.'?

_____ shouted 'Hamid is our best player.'

3   Who scored the first goal?

_____

_____

4   Who scored just before the end of the first half?

_____

_____

5   How was Hamid feeling at half time?

_____

_____

6   Why do you think Hamid carried on playing when he didn't feel well?

_____

_____

Writing a story

Imagine that you were in Hamid and William's school play of The Pied Piper of Hamelin. Which part would you like to take? The play is going really well when suddenly William's pet mouse, which he had in his pocket, escapes and runs across the stage. What happens next? Write the story.

_____

_____

_____

_____

_____

_____

_____

_____

Putting in order

Here are some events in the story. Write out the sentences in the correct order. The first one is done for you.

Trevor Kent tripped over.
His basket of plastic chops and sausages went flying into the audience.
The music started and the curtain went up.
The audience laughed and laughed.
The children playing the part of the townspeople did a dance.
Some of the dancers tripped over Trevor.

1   The music started and the curtain went up.

2   _____

_____

3   _____

_____

4   _____

_____

5   _____

_____

6   _____

_____

Thinking about the story

Using pages 14–16 of the story

1   Who was at the front of the hall sitting around a big table?

     At the front of the hall, around a big table sat _____

     _____.

2   Who was the man dressed in brightly coloured clothes?

     The man dressed in brightly coloured clothes was _____

     _____.

3   What was on the table?

     _____

     _____

4   Who did the Pied Piper shake hands with?

     _____

     _____

5   What sort of tune did the Pied Piper play on his magic pipe?

     _____

     _____

6   Why do you think the Mayor held on to the bag of gold?

     _____

     _____

Writing a letter

You have read the story of William and the Pied Piper. Imagine that you are the Mayor of Hamelin and that you are writing a letter to the Pied Piper asking him to help you get rid of all the rats in the town. You need to tell him all about the trouble the rats have been causing. These words may help you.

houses	terrible	everywhere	gold
worried	buildings	townspeople	noise

The Town Hall
Market Square
Hamelin

Dear Mr Pied Piper,

_____

_____

_____

_____

_____

_____

Yours sincerely,

Mr Mayor

Finding information

Here is a poster for a musical play of the Pied Piper of Hamelin at a local theatre. Read it carefully and then answer the questions below.

The Pied Piper of Hamelin

at

The King's Theatre, Thespian Street

Friday 2nd April at 7.30

Music by Carmen Listen

starring

Terry Bulltune as the Pied Piper and

Ivor Lottamoney as the Mayor and

children from Gospel Oak School as the rats

Children – £1.30   Adults – £3.00

Tickets from the Box Office – telephone 0171 923 260

1   Which theatre is the play being performed in? _____

2   Which street is the theatre in? _____

3   When is the play? _____

4   What time does the play start? _____

5   How much does it cost for children to see the play? _____

6   Who wrote the music? _____

7   Who is playing the part of the Mayor? _____

8   If you want a ticket for this play, what telephone number do you need to ring? _____

_____.

Thinking about the story

Using pages 16–21 of the story

1 Who was getting ready for the Jump Up?

_____ were getting ready for the Jump Up.

2 What is a 'Jump Up'?

A 'Jump Up' is another name for a _____.

3 Who made Wilf and Wilma's costumes for the Jump Up?

_____

_____

4 What did Wilf do at the Jump Up?

_____

_____

5 What do you think Grandfather meant when he said 'My Jump Up days are over.'?

_____

_____

6 What sort of clothes did people wear for the Jump Up?

_____

_____

Writing a story

These people were really enjoying their holiday. The sun was shining and they were all able to do lots of different things. Imagine that you were there too when suddenly ... the sky grew dark, the wind blew stronger and the sea became rough. A storm was coming! Describe what happened.

_____

_____

_____

_____

_____

_____

_____

Writing a postcard

Wilf and Wilma wrote a postcard to Biff, Chip and Kipper.

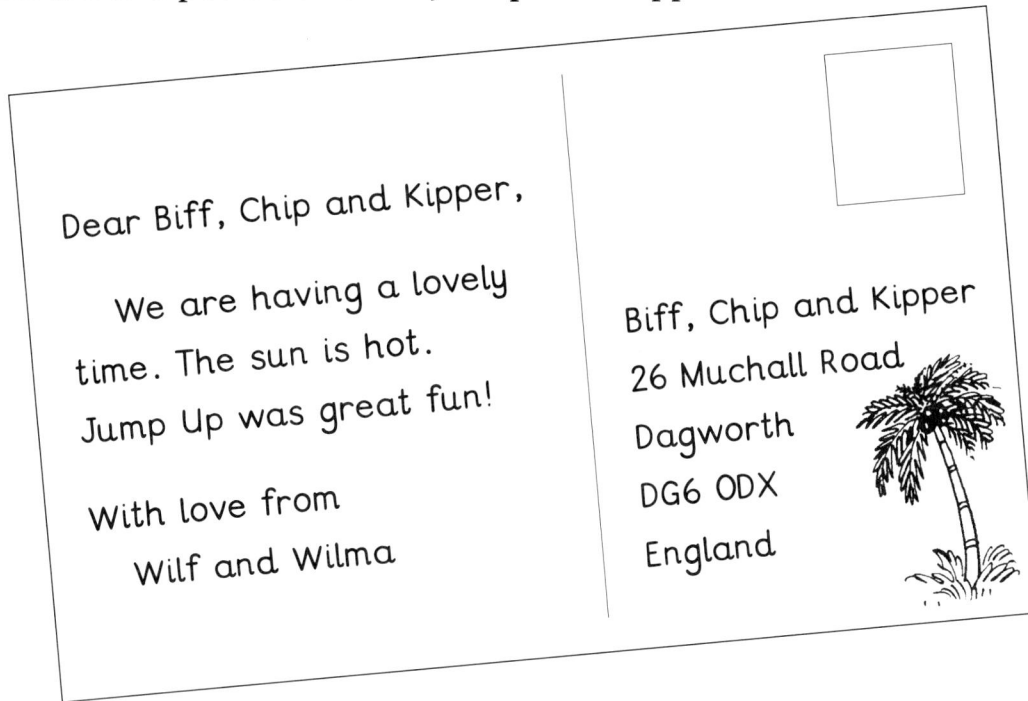

Dear Biff, Chip and Kipper,

We are having a lovely time. The sun is hot. Jump Up was great fun!

With love from
Wilf and Wilma

Biff, Chip and Kipper
26 Muchall Road
Dagworth
DG6 ODX
England

Have you been on holiday or been for a day visit somewhere exciting? Write a postcard to your mum, dad, grandparents or a friend. Tell them what you have been doing. Remember to write the address on the right hand side.

Dear _____ ,

_____

_____

_____

_____

_____

_____

_____

_____

_____

_____

Thinking about the story

Using pages 16–18 of the story

1   Where had Anneena's group gone?

Anneena's group had gone to the _____.

2   What were Wilf, Wilma, Nadim and Biff doing?

Wilf and Wilma were_____

_____ and Nadim and Biff were _____

_____.

3   What was Chip trying to find out?

_____

_____

_____

4   What did the keeper tell Chip that tigers like to eat?

_____

_____

_____

5   Do you think that the zoo keeper was joking? Why do you think that?

_____

_____

_____

6   Why was Mr Johnson looking worried?

_____

_____

_____

Writing a story

Write a story about a secret present. Think about a secret present that you bought for someone. (Perhaps you made it for them?) Who was it for? Why did it have to be a secret? What size was it? Where did you hide it? Was the person pleased?

_____

_____

_____

_____

_____

_____

_____

Filling in gaps

Read the words in the passage, then try to fill in the gaps with the word that you think fits best.

The coach arrived to take the class to the _____.

Before they got in, Mr Johnson spoke to them.

'_____ last zoo trip was spoilt by the rain,' he _____.

'This time nothing will go wrong.'

'When can we _____ our sandwiches?' asked Chip.

'No eating until lunchtime,' said _____ Johnson.

'Work in groups,' he said, 'and find out _____ you can about your

favourite animal.

Draw a picture _____ it and find out what it likes to eat.'

'_____ wonder if tigers like ham sandwiches,' said Chip.

Using adjectives

Describing words (adjectives) make a story more interesting. Choose the describing word that you think best fits the gaps in the sentences below.

very important	big	terrible

little	huge	favourite

1   One evening they found one of the offices in a _____ mess.

2   Anneena picked up some _____ pieces of white paper.

3   The man had lost some _____ plans.

4   'I must have given them to the _____ girl.'

5   He had a _____ piece of meat on a wheelbarrow.

6   'You will be able to finish your work on your _____ animal,' said Mr Johnson.

Thinking about the story

Using pages 30–32 of the story

1   What did the ghosts do that night?

That night the ghosts _____

_____.

2   Who were the guests of honour?

_____ were the guests of honour.

3   What was the best game of all?

_____

_____

4   What was the house turned into?

_____

_____

5   Why do you think it was difficult playing Hide-and-Seek with a family of ghosts?

_____

_____

_____

6   Why do you think that only Ann and Jess saw the ghosts?

_____

_____

_____

Writing a story

Imagine that, like Ann and Jess, you have a young friend who is a ghost. He likes to follow you everywhere you go. Unfortunately, one day he follows you to school! Tell the story of what happened.

_____

_____

_____

_____

_____

_____

_____

_____

_____

_____

_____

_____

_____

_____

_____

_____

_____

_____

Filling in gaps

Read the words in the passage, then try to fill in the gaps with the word that you think fits best.

Horton was a small but beautiful village. In its _____ stood a very old

manor house. Nobody had lived _____ for many years and it had just been

sold _____ a new owner. The villagers hoped it would become _____

local museum.

Ann and Jess were in the same _____ at school.

'Today,' said Miss Murphy, 'we are all _____ to the old manor house to

paint pictures of _____. It's going to be knocked down soon and I

_____ you all to have something to remember it by.'

Using adjectives

Describing words (adjectives) make a story more interesting. Choose the word which best fits the gaps in the sentences.

good	beautiful	creaking

old	old-fashioned	strange

1   Horton was a small but _____ village.

2   'But they can't knock down the _____ house,' said Ann.

3   'I should be able to take some _____ photos here,' said Jess.

4   They could see a huge, _____ kitchen.

5   'What _____ clothes they're wearing,' said Jess.

6   It swung open with a loud _____ sound.

Thinking about the story

Using pages 1–5 of the story

1   How long had it been raining for?

It had been raining for _____.

2   Amy's parents had two businesses. What were they?

Amy's parents owned a _____

and a _____.

3   What did Mum say that they'd have to do if things didn't get any better?

_____

_____

_____

4   Did Amy want to live in a town?

_____

5   Why didn't Amy want to live in a town?

_____

_____

_____

6   Mrs Long was an archaeologist. What does an archaeologist do?

_____

_____

_____

Writing a story

You are helping Mum and Dad to dig a big hole in the garden where you are going to have a pond. While you are working your spade hits something hard. What happens next? Have you found something from long ago? Some of the words below may help you.

_____

_____

_____

_____

_____

_____

_____

_____

_____

_____

_____

_____

_____

_____

_____

_____

| beautiful | excited | treasure | dirty |
| archaeologist | surprise | digging | old |

Using full stops and capital letters

Amy wrote this letter to her grandparents telling them all about Mrs Long and finding the Roman villa. She forgot to put in all the full stops and capital letters. Will you put them in for her? You will need to read the letter carefully. You could use a red crayon to show where the full stops and capital letters should go. We have done the first few for you.

Remember that you need a capital letter for the beginning of a sentence and for the name of a place or a person.

The Roman Villa Caravan Site

Llanedran

Pembrokeshire

Wales

Thursday 3rd August

Dear grandma and grandpa,

we have had a very exciting week it rained and rained all week mrs long, the archaeologist, came to stay again we went for a walk mum came to fetch us in the landrover but the bridge broke and the landrover sank in the mud the river bank collapsed when it stopped raining we found some old jars in the river bank and some roman mosaics mrs long says that they are part of a roman villa lots of people have come to see it and the caravan park is full

see you soon

lots of love

amy

xxxxxx

Further activities

Many different themes and topics are covered by the stories in *Oxford Reading Tree*. This section contains ideas for developing three of these topics so as to provide a framework for a variety of cross-curricular activities.

Caring for and helping others

The following *Oxford Reading Tree* books could be read as part of this topic:

The Dump, William and the dog, The emergency, Kate and the sheep (Robins); *Max makes breakfast, The surprise* (More Robins)

'People who help us' is a common theme for study at Key Stage 1. It normally includes all those people who help us at home, at school and in the community. This can be broadened to include children helping others: helping at home, helping at school, helping elderly people, helping those with disabilities, helping others in need in the world; looking after pets; looking after the environment and caring for ourselves – health, hygiene and safety.

Language

Families: You could use *Max makes breakfast* to talk about people in the family who care for us – parents, grandparents, uncles, aunts, older brothers and sisters. There may be other people who care for us too, such as neighbours and childminders. Talk about Max and Kerry's grandad and encourage the children to recount occasions when their grandparents have helped them like Max and Kerry's did. Ask the children to think of some of the special things they have done with their families, places they have visited and presents they have received. Ask the children to write thank you letters to family members.

People in the community: Talk about the people in the community who help us. What about the people in the school? The children could invite other teachers, dinner supervisors, the caretaker, secretary, lollipop lady/man, to come and talk about their work. What they say could be recorded in large speech bubbles for display.

The children could write letters of invitation to various people in the community who help or care, such as school nurses, dentists, policemen or policewomen. Discuss what information should be included in a letter which asks people to visit the school and talk to the children about their job. The children could then decide upon questions that they would wish to ask the visitor(s) and who is going to ask what. The interview(s) could be taped and played back later encouraging the children to extract information for further work and to evaluate their own performances.

Saying sorry: Discuss how Kate and Jo felt in *Kate and the sheep* when they let the sheep out. The children might want to talk about times when they had tried to help but something had gone wrong. Kate and Jo said that they were sorry but they could also have written a letter. Discuss the layout of such a letter. The children could then write a letter from Kate or Jo to Mr Munday saying sorry.

Science

Using *The surprise* and *Kate and the sheep*, discuss the needs of a new-born animal. Are they different from those of a human baby? Use the children's experiences and those of Ben, Kate and Jo to build up a list of 'Dos and Don'ts' for people looking after new-born animals and human babies. Encourage the children to see the similarities between caring for pets and humans.

The children could volunteer information about pets and collect more from other people, for example: What sort of pets do you have? What does your pet need? (Food, water, warmth and exercise.) How often do you feed your pet? exercise your pet? change its bedding? Following on from this you could encourage the children to write 'A step by step guide to looking after a pet' using words and pictures. A local vet could be invited to talk to the children about pet care.

When discussing the basic life requirements of animals and people, you could talk about William's dislike of keeping fit in *William's mistake*. Make a list of all the different ways in which the children or their parents keep fit. Why is keeping fit important? William says that he'd like to watch television all day. Discuss this with the children. The children could create a collage of different forms of exercise.

Maths

Use the information collected about class pets to make a large pictogram of the pets owned by the children in the class or which the children know. Individually, transfer this information into another pictogram (perhaps using a template to ensure regular sizes) or block graph. A 3D version of the block graph could be made by using construction blocks standing on pictures of each pet. More advanced mathematicians could use a tally system to collect information from a number of classes thereby handling larger numbers. Use a simple database on the computer to present the same information in a variety of forms.

Similar data handling work could be done using William's love of television in *William's mistake* as a stimulus. Collect information on how much time the children spend watching television. A pie chart of how each of them spends the 24 hours in a day could be constructed. How much time is spent doing some kind of exercise? How much time sleeping? How much time eating?

Geography

Talk about *The emergency* as a good introduction to the work of the emergency services (Police, Ambulance, Fire). Discuss the different services and their work. What does their work entail? Encourage the children to talk about any experiences they may have had seeing or using the emergency services. Talk about how to make emergency phone calls. (Many local services, with plenty of notice, are only too happy to bring their appliances into schools and explain their work.)

If you are inviting people into the school to talk about the work they do you could enlarge a map of your local area and plot where some of these people are based. Ask the children questions, such as 'How far away is your doctor's surgery?' 'Do you walk there or do you go by car or bus?'.

Using the book *Kate and the sheep*, discuss The Country Code. What is it? Why is it important? Why is litter a danger to animals? Why is it important to shut gates behind you? Using a word processor, help the

children to design their own poster promoting The Country Code.

Art

A welcoming display in the entrance area of the school is a valuable project to work on. The children can take photographs, draw and paint portraits of all the staff (teaching and non-teaching) and others like the school nurse who help them, forming a 'Who's who in our school'. Apart from being attractive and welcoming, it would also be very useful for visitors to the school!

Design Technology

The children could design a safe playground. What are the possible dangers in a playground? What should be included? They could design a layout and/or make a model.

RE

Encourage the children to talk about the many people who care for them and how they can care for others. Discuss how Jesus taught people to care through parables such as The good Samaritan or The prodigal son. There are many stories from the life and teaching of Mohammed about the belief that all small creatures and animals are the creation of Allah and must be treated with care and kindness. 'Ahisma' is a basic Hindu belief which means not harming any living things. Many Buddhists make a daily vow not to harm any living thing. The story of Prince Siddharta and the Swan is a Buddhist story demonstrating this belief.

Book list

Story books

Allan Ahlberg *Cops and robbers* (Picture Lions, Armada Books)
Vivien Alcock *Wait and see* (Toppers, Belitha)
Leila Berg *My dog Sunday* (Young Puffin)
John Burningham *Grandpa – the book of the film* (Red Fox)
Babette Cole *The trouble with – Mum, Dad, Gran* (Picture Lions)
Gina *Horace the dragon has toothache* (Book Bus, Collins)
Nigel Gray *Carrot top* (Young Lions)
Mwenye Hadithi *Greedy zebra* (Picture Knight, Hodder and Stoughton)
Mairi Hedderwick *Katie Morag delivers the mail* (Picture Lions)
Shirley Hughes *Dogger* (Bodley Head)
Pat Hutchins *You'll soon grow into them, Titch* (Picture Puffins)
Rose Impey and Jolyne Knox *Houdini dog* (Jets, Young Lions)
Shirley Isherwood *Alice alone* (Macdonald)
Dick King-Smith *Yob* (Heinemann)
Nigel McMullen *Lucky – the story of a puppy* (Heinemann)

Hilary Sharpe *Adelaide's naughty Granny* (Mammoth)

Poetry books
From the *Oxford Reading Tree*
People poems (More Acorns)

Other poetry books
John Agard *I din do nuttin* (Puffin)

Information books
Dorothy Baldwin & Claire Lister, *Safety in the home, Safety on the road, Safety at school* (Safety First, Wayland)
Diana Bentley *The School Secretary, Dinner Ladies, The School Caretaker, The Lollipop Man* (My School, Wayland)
Roger Coote and Diana Bentley *My little sister, My big brother, My parents, My grandparents,* (My Family, Firefly)
Brian and Gillian Cutting *Animal pets* (Sunshine, Heinemann)
Wayne Jackman, *Healthy teeth, Healthy hair, Healthy skin, Healthy eyes, Healthy hands and feet, Healthy eating* (Healthy Living, Wayland)
T Nutkin *Pets* (BBC)

Jill Brand with Wendy Blow and Caroline Short *The green umbrella* (WWF and A C Black). This contains stories, songs, poems and starting points for environmental assemblies. It emphasises the great similarity in the attitudes of the world's religions to man's responsibility to care for his environment.

Schools

The following *Oxford Reading Tree* books could be read as part of this topic:

The old vase, The photograph, The secret plans (Robins);
William's mistake, Hamid does his best, William and the Pied Piper (More Robins)

This topic can have a strong history bias exploring the difference between schools in the past and the present. *The photograph* is an ideal introduction into this aspect of the topic. Many 'living museums' have school rooms where children can dress up and experience at first hand a school room in the Victorian or Edwardian period.

Language

School visits: You could use *The secret plans* as a starting point for this. What do you need to do to prepare for a visit? If you are organizing a visit to a 'living museum' as part of this topic, involve the children in all areas of planning, such as writing letters to arrange the visit and letters to parents with permission slips; making lists of children, staff and helpers going and of items to be taken; confirming coach times and writing thank you letters following the visit. On return ask the children to describe their day. Ask them to tell others about their day in written form or in the form of a class assembly to parents and children. Using a video camera, some of them could present a 'News Item' on the visit.

Designing a prospectus: Ask the whole class to design a prospectus for your school in the form of a 'big class book'. Ask groups to be responsible for specific areas. Talk about the range of information required. What would a new child and his/her parents need to know? Illustrations of specific rooms, people, uniform (if applicable), school plays, sports day, and visits could be included. Discuss the need for a contents page.

Writing diaries: Ask the children to write a diary for a week. Discuss diaries. What are they for? Why are they so important to historians?

Maths

Collect information from the class on how the children travel to school. Present the results in a pictogram and then a block graph. (A simple database such as Our Facts can be used for this.) Ask for parents' help in timing the children's journeys to school. Who has the longest journey? Who has the shortest journey? Some children could borrow a trundle wheel and, with the aid of an adult, could measure the distance. Others could borrow a stop watch and time the journey. A large map of the local area could be displayed showing where children live and their relative distances from the school. This could be contrasted with information gathered from staff, many of whom will travel to school by car or bus and sometimes from quite a distance.

Science

Ask the children to bring in photographs of themselves as babies and toddlers. How have they changed? What can they do now that they couldn't do then? How much have they grown? They could list the physical changes which have taken place since they were babies.

Collect data from the class on height, shoe size and hand size. (Be sensitive to the children's feelings when doing work which relates to individual differences.) If feasible, engage the help of Year 6 pupils in collecting similar data for their class. The children can then make comparisons. The simple data base, Our Facts, could be used to record this information.

History

A number of schools have collections of photographs from the past. They make a wonderful historical record of the past life of the school. These photographs can be displayed in their decades in a large time-line around the classroom. The children can add pictures of cars, fashion and important happenings in the news for those decades. Photographs of themselves and other members of their family can be added in the decade in which they were born.

The children could compare one of the class photographs of the past with one of their own class. What are the differences? You could try to contact an ex-pupil and ask them to talk to the children about school life when they were young.

With the children's help you could compile a questionnaire to send home to adult family members asking them about their school life. Information could include: We started school at ..., For lunch I had ..., I wore ..., My favourite lesson was ..., I got to school by ..., I liked to sing ....

Using *The photograph* talk about schools in Victorian times. A visit to a 'living' museum where they have a school room would be ideal. What were the differences? Clothes? Subjects? Buildings? What was the drill? How old were the children when they started school? You could arrange a Victorian day when the staff and children dress in clothes of the period and have lessons in Victorian style. You will need to rearrange the classroom furniture to create a more formal layout.

Geography

Read *The photograph* and encourage the children to look carefully at the differences between William's classroom now and in Victorian times. What differences in terms of layout, furniture, lighting, decoration, can they see? Ask the children to draw a plan of their own classroom. (It helps to work together on one large class one first.) Then, by using *The photograph*, try to draw a plan of William's classroom in Victorian times. Comparing the two in detail is easier if the children put a grid over their plans. What can you see in a particular square? Ask the children to give a grid location for the bookcase, the door, etc. (You could photocopy grids onto overhead projector acetates.)

The children could draw a plan of the school. Explore the use of symbols for these plans. Using the plan, the children could design a school trail. Where would you take someone who wanted to look at your school? Try to avoid doubling back too much. You could then invite a governor in to the school to try out the trail.

Design Technology

Ask the children to look carefully at the plans of the classroom that they have drawn up in Geography. Ask them to make a model of the classroom and furniture using either construction kits or junk materials. Encourage the children to look at relative sizes, for example, the size of the table in relation to the door.

Art

The children could make a collection of rubbings from around the school, for example, hall floor, playground surface, wooden bench, brickwork, tree bark, manhole cover. Cut them into tiles and by alternating colour, display on one piece of paper.

The children could draw parts of the school, for example, the entrance, the playground, the hall. Portraits of 'People in my school' could be painted. They could be displayed next to a photograph taken by the children.

Music

Ask each member of staff to name their favourite piece of music. Let the children listen to it and talk about it. Do you like it too? Would you like to dance to it? Curl up and sleep to it? What instruments can you hear? Is there a strong beat? Is it fast? slow? loud? soft?

A questionnaire asking family members what is their favourite music to relax to, dance to and do jobs to, can provide you with some very interesting information, for example, 'This is Sam's grandad's favourite music. Do you like it Sam? Why/Why not?'

Book list

Story books
Allan Ahlberg and Faith Jacques *Mr Tick the Teacher* (Kestrel)
Janet and Allan Ahlberg *The great marathon football match* (Picture Lions)
Althea *The school fair* (Cambridge University Press)
Bernard Ashley *Dinner ladies don't count* (Julia Macrae/Blackbird)
Nick Butterworth and Mick Inkpen *Sports day* (Hodder & Stoughton)
Gillian Cross *Save our school* (Methuen)

Roald Dahl *Matilda* (Puffin)
Heather Eyles *The trouble with Herbert* (Red Fox)
Anne Fine *Only a show* (Young Puffin)
Rumer Godden *Diddakoi* (Penguin)
Shirley Hughes *Lucy and Tom go to school* (Carousel Books)
Shirley Hughes *Angel Mae* (Walker Books)
Pat Hutchins *Follow that bus* (Lions)
Margaret Joy *Tales from Allotment Lane School* (Young Puffin)
Rob Lewis *Ollie's song* (Simon and Schuster)
Colin McNaughton *Football crazy* (Mammoth)
Chris Powling and Scoular Anderson *Hiccup Harry* (Jets, Young Lions)

Poetry books
From the *Oxford Reading Tree*
School Poems (Conkers)

Other poetry books
Allen Ahlberg *Heard it in the playground* (Puffin)
Allen Ahlberg *Please Mrs Butler* (Puffin)
Stanley Cook 'In the playground' *Another second poetry book* edited by John Foster (Oxford University Press)
John Foster *School's out* (Oxford University Press)
Julie Holder 'Playground count' *Another second poetry book* edited by John Foster (Oxford University Press)

Information books
From the *Oxford Reading Tree Fact Finders*
Schools (More Unit C – published 1997)

Other information books
Diana Bentley *The school fete* (Wayland)
Anne Cibardi and Stephen Cartwright *Going to school* (First experiences, Usborne)
Clive Pace and Jean Birch *Look around the school* (Wayland)
Stewart Ross *Our schools* (Starting history, Wayland)
Monica Stoppleman *School day* (A C Black)
Richard Wood *A Victorian school* (Wayland)

Plays
Gene Kem *The turbulent term of Tyke Tyler* (Oxford University Press)

Holidays and visits

The following *Oxford Reading Tree* books could be read as part of this topic:

The holiday, A proper bike, The village show (Robins); *The long journey, Mum's new car, Treasure hunt, Ghost tricks, The discovery* (More Robins)

This topic can provide a wealth of opportunities to explore geography. Staff and pupils at the school can help by bringing back photographs from their holidays. Establish before they go the type that you need, for

example, a place of worship, a post office, a telephone box, a post box, a 'typical' house, supermarket, types of transport, an elderly 'local' and a young 'local', a policeman ...

A school collection will soon build up, providing an excellent basis for work encouraging children to look at similarities and differences.

Language
Postcards: The class could make a collection of postcards. Talk about the types of things you would write on a postcard and the layout of addresses. Ask the children to write postcards to their family describing a holiday or visit. The photocopiable language activity on page 115 for *The holiday* provides a postcard layout. This may be easier to tackle first. Using *The long journey* the children could write a postcard from Kerry to a friend describing her holiday. The children could cut up holiday brochures to make pictures for the front of their postcards.

Holiday adverts: Collect posters and advertisements for holidays (in newspapers, magazines and travel brochures) and discuss them with the children. What information is included? The children could design a poster for Amy's parents' Caravan Park in *The discovery*.

Travel shop: You could turn the home corner into a travel agent's shop. Ask a local travel agent for some posters and brochures. Make some simplified booking forms for them to complete, for example, name, address, destination, dates, type of accommodation. Obtain particulars on local areas of interest, local coach tours and information on a particularly popular seaside destination for people in your area. A simplified local map and world map displayed will help the children to begin to locate various destinations.

Holiday diary: Ask the children to write an account in the form of a diary of a holiday or visit they have been on. Children with limited holiday experience could write about a visit like William's in *Treasure hunt* or Ann and Jess's in *Ghost tricks*, a family wedding as in *Mum's new car*, or a bike ride with friends as in *A proper bike*.

Science
Weather is obviously an integral part of work on holidays and visits. Look at the weather in *The holiday* and *The discovery*. Discuss how it affects the characters

involved. Monitor the weather for a month and look at patterns. What sort of clouds usually give rain? Are the clouds high or low? Encourage the children to make up their own weather symbols, then introduce them to established standard symbols for weather. Watch a weather forecast together on the television. Using a simple map and symbols, ask the children to present a weather forecast. Perhaps they could present the one that Wilf and Wilma's grandfather saw on the television and you could record it using a video camera?

Maths

Make a seaside kiosk in the classroom, selling rock, ice-creams, lollies and candy floss. Give the children practice at buying and selling. Alternatively create a provisions store similar to Amy's in *The discovery*. What sort of things do caravan holiday-makers need? How much would they cost? The children could be given duplicated shopping lists with which to go to the shop. The children could find out the prices of the goods and write them down on the list in the form of a sum. These could be either added using a calculator or without, depending on ability. To assist less able children you could stick the correct plastic coins to the item, next to the price, so that it becomes a matching exercise.

History

Looking at *Treasure hunt* and *Ghost tricks*, discuss similar local places of historic interest. If possible arrange a visit to one. There is a wealth of information in the illustrations accompanying both these stories and there would be much to gain from looking at these together, for example, looking at buildings, costumes, pastimes, food, etc. Children could use 'I Spy' to investigate and explore the illustrations further, for example, 'I spy a strange suit of clothes made from metal and used to fight in'. Continue until they find the page number and the name. Discussion on each object will be spontaneous.

Geography

Look at a map of the United Kingdom together. Where have you visited? Look at a map of the world together. Where have you or your family or friends visited? Collect postcards and holiday snaps and attach to countries of origin on the world and United Kingdom map. Where do people stay? – bed and breakfast, hotels, guest houses, tents, caravans, holiday camps, cottages. Look at the differences. How do people travel? – train, coach, car, plane, ferry, hovercraft, cruiser.

You might want to investigate a holiday locality outside the United Kingdom as a contrasting locality. *The holiday* would make a good introduction to the Caribbean. Within the UK a contrasting locality, such as seaside, market town, industrial town, could be explored with a class visit to introduce the area.

Discuss the problems faced by the villagers in *Ghost tricks*. Who do the children think was right – Mr Simon Smart or the villagers? Give some balance to the argument by asking where villagers without cars would be able to buy their groceries. Small village shops tend to be more expensive than big supermarkets. Is all development bad? There may be a local development in progress that the children can explore further.

Design Technology

The children could design and make a beach bag for Wilf or Wilma. Demonstrate planning by drawing a plan of the bag, listing its functions, materials needed and ideas for decoration. What are its functions? Do you need it to be waterproof? Look at its strengths and weaknesses. Can you get everything in?

Music

Discuss the storm in *The holiday* and the sequence of weather conditions in a storm. Listen to some 'stormy' music. (Arnold Bax's 'Tintagel' is a good example and an ideal length.)

Use body sounds (blowing, whistling, clapping, fingers tapping, feet tapping and stamping) as a class to create a sequence entitled 'Storm'. Establish groups for calm ripples of waves, seagulls, wind, rain and thunder and lightning. Discuss dynamics. When should it be loud? When should it be soft? Who should begin first?

Following on from this, use percussion instruments in groups to create the sounds and shape of the storm. This is best done as a class composition again with the teacher directing who plays when. The children from the previously established groups will choose the instrument they think best creates that sound. From this the children will then have enough experience to create their own 'Sea storm' compositions in groups. They can make their own scores to show what happens when, as at the top of the next page.

A conductor can direct by moving her hand across the score. Each child commences playing when she sees her symbol and finishes playing when she sees the symbol repeated.

Art

Encourage the children to talk about the statue of Cupid in *Treasure hunt*. Explain its origins and how popular statues have been for centuries. They were used for decoration in houses and gardens in the past, to commemorate famous people and as a focus for religious worship. Draw the children's attention to any local statues. They could also collect pictures of famous statues. Using plasticine, ask the children to make a model of a statue – it could be of themselves. Mount them on plinths (you could use wooden or plastic building blocks) to give them stability and the authentic look!

The children could design and paint a bright beach towel for Wilf or Wilma. Think of bright, 'summery' colours. These look most effective displayed on a 'washing line' across the classroom.

RE

You could discuss the idea of religious pilgrimages with the children, mentioning Mecca, Jerusalem, Lourdes, Benares, Amritsar, Canterbury, Lindisfarne. Ask a parent or teacher who has been on a pilgrimage to share their experience with the children.

Book list

Story books
From the *Oxford Reading Tree*
Lucky the goat (*More Sparrows* Stage 4); *The outing* (*Owls* Stage 6)

Other story books
Michael Bond *A day by the sea* (Picture Lions)
Olivia Bennett *A busy weekend* (Hamish Hamilton)
Celia Berridge *What did you do in the holidays?* (Andre Deutsch)
Terrance Dicks *T R afloat* (Young Corgi)
Keith Faulkner *Sam at the seaside* (Beehive Books)
Anne Fine *A sudden swirl of icy wind* (Mammoth)
Grace Hallworth *The carnival kite* (Methuen)
Janosch *The trip to Panama* (Anderson Press)
Evan Jones *Anansi stories*, *Stories from History*, *The Beginning of Things*, *Witches and Duppies* (Tales of the Caribbean, Ginn)
Margaret Joy *Allotment Lane in London* (Young Puffin)
Dick King-Smith *Friends and brothers* (Mammoth)
Sheila Lavelle *Holiday with The Fiend* (Young Lions)
Sheila Lavelle *Ursula camping* (Young Corgi)
Errol Lloyd *Nini at carnival* (Bodley Head)
Phillipa Pearce *Tom's midnight garden* (Puffin)
Lance Salway *The haunting of Hemlock Hall* (Young Corgi)
Joan Solomon *A day by the sea* (Look I'm reading series, Hamish Hamilton)
Margaret Stuart *Barry the Witch on holiday* (Fontana/Young Lions)
Jill Tomlinson *The cat who wanted to go home* (Magnet, Methuen)
How Ackee and Saltfish became Friends, *Anansi and the Green Banana*, *Anansi, Turtle and Pigeon*, *The Magic Pot*, *The Hat Shaking Festival*, *The Story of Ti Suki*, *The Fishing Trip and Frangipani and Maroni* (Share a Story, Ginn)

Poetry books
From the *Oxford Reading Tree*
Holiday Poems (*Catkins*)
Special Days Poems (*Catkins*)
Seasons Poems (*Catkins*)
Weather Poems (*Conkers*)
Sea Poems (*Jackdaws* poetry)

Other poetry books
John Foster *Let's celebrate* (Oxford University Press)

Information books
John Caldwell *Let's visit the West Indies* (Macmillan)
Anne Civardi and Stephen Cartwright *Going on a plane* (First experiences, Usborne)
Stewart Ross *Our holidays* (Starting history, Wayland)
Ruth Thompson *The seaside* (Changing Times, Franklin Watts)
Sheila Watson *A Victorian holiday* (Victorian Life, Wayland)

Oxford Reading Tree: Robins storybooks

Name . . . . Date started . . . .

Date completed . . . .

Robins and More Robins	Date	Comments
Robins		
The Dump		
The old vase		
William and the dog		
The emergency		
Kate and the sheep		
The photograph		
The village show		
A proper bike		
The holiday		
The secret plans		
More Robins		
Max makes breakfast		
The long journey		
Mum's new car		
The surprise		
William's mistake		
Treasure hunt		
Hamid does his best		
William and the Pied Piper		
Ghost tricks		
The discovery		

**Oxford
Reading
Tree**

Name . . . .

Date . . . .

Running record sheet
from *Robins* Stage 6 *The Dump* pages 20–22

Introduction

Talk about the story so far: What had The Dump been like? How had it become a building site? What had Lenny done to try and get another place to play? Why was the little playground no good for children like Lenny and his friends?

We didn't play in the new playground.

We painted a goal on the fence of The

  Dump and played in the street.

Then Tracey kicked the ball too high and

  it went over the fence.

The building site was locked up, but

  I wanted to see where my ball was.

104 words

'My brother can get it tomorrow,' I said.

  'Give me a leg up and I'll have a look.'

I looked over the fence.

I saw my ball, but I saw something else.

Two men were loading things on to a lorry.

I didn't want the men to see me, so

  I jumped down quickly.

1 How did they lose the ball over the fence?
2 Why did Lenny climb up to look over the fence?
3 How do you know that it was in the evening?
4 Why didn't Lenny want the men to see him?
5 What word in the passage means the same as 'putting' or 'stacking'?

Retelling

Types of miscues/reading strategies . . . .

Number of words read accurately   ☐   Percentage accuracy   ☐

**Oxford
Reading
Tree**

Name . . . .

Date . . . .

Running record sheet

from *More Robins* Stage 7 *The long journey* pages 16–18

Introduction

Talk about the car journey. Who is going? Where are they going? What problems have they had so far on the journey? Why did they have to stop at the service station? Why do you think Dad looks so worried?

Soon they were driving down narrow

country lanes. It was still raining but most

of the traffic had gone.

'We'll be fine now,' smiled Dad. 'I'm sure the

cottage is just at the end of this lane.'

'Yes, I remember this bit from last year,'

said Mum.

Kerry looked out of the window.

105 words

'I don't remember this lane,' she thought, but

she didn't say anything to Mum and Dad.

'Where's Bubbles?' asked Max quietly.

There was a farm gate at the end of the lane.

'I think we may have taken a wrong turn,'

said Mum.

'I feel sick,' moaned Kerry.

'Bubbles gone!' screamed Max.

1 What was the weather like?
2 Where did Dad think the cottage was?
3 Why do you think Kerry decided not to tell Mum and Dad that she didn't remember the lane?
4 Why was Max upset?
5 What word in the passage means the same as 'said' but in a sad and complaining voice?

Retelling

Types of miscues/reading strategies . . . .

Number of words read accurately

Percentage accuracy

Oxford Reading Tree

Name . . . .

Date . . . .

Running record sheet
from *More Robins* Stage 9 *Treasure hunt* pages 6–8

Introduction

Talk about the 'Children's Day' at Grondale Hall. What was it? Discuss what William and Hamid had done so far. Who had won a prize? Who had been unpleasant to William and Hamid?

A voice came over the loudspeakers. It said:

'The treasure hunt is about to start.

Everyone wanting to take part please go to

the steps of the big house.'

'Let's go,' said Hamid. 'It sounds like fun.'

Lord Grondale himself read out the rules.

'You have to look for two envelopes,' he said.

108 words

'The first one is in the house. It tells you

where to find the second one. If you find

the second one, you've won the prize.'

'There's no point in trying to cheat,' he

said. 'You'll never find the second envelope

if you haven't read the first. So off you go

into the house. Good luck!'

1 What is a loudspeaker?
2 Where did everyone have to meet who was taking part in the treasure hunt?
3 Who read out the rules to everyone?
4 How many envelopes were there?
5 Why wasn't there any point in trying to cheat?

Retelling

Types of miscues/reading strategies . . . .

Number of words read accurately

Percentage accuracy

**Oxford
Reading
Tree**

Name . . . .

Date . . . .

Running record sheet

from *Robins* Stage 10 *The holiday* pages 25–27

Introduction

Talk about the sudden rain at the Jump Up. Discuss how Grandfather had heard that a bad storm was coming and talk about why he was worried.

The wind had begun to blow and the sky

  had turned a deep grey.

The grandparents began putting shutters up

  at all the windows.

'You can help,' Grandfather told Wilf and

  Wilma. 'Help put these shutters up.'

The next day, the storm hit the island.

The house shook as the wind beat into it,

  and the rain lashed against it.

Great waves rolled in from the sea.

Trees blew down and some of the houses

  had their roofs blown off.

Wilf and Wilma were frightened by the storm.

One of the shutters flew open and things

  crashed and banged against the house.

'Don't worry,' said Grandfather. 'Storms

  like this don't last for long.'

'I hope the house won't blow away,' said Wilf.

102 words

1 What signs were there that a storm was coming?
2 How did the grandparents protect the house?
3 Why do you think Wilf and Wilma were so frightened?
4 What was the worst thing that happened during the storm?
5 What other word in the passage means the same as 'beat'?

Retelling

Types of miscues/reading strategies . . . .

Number of words read accurately

Percentage accuracy

JACKDAWS Stages 8–11

Jackdaws and More Jackdaws anthologies

Jackdaws		More Jackdaws	
The spoilt holiday	*Kate's garden*	*The school play*	*The playroom*
Anna's eggs	*In the snow*	*The jokers*	*The snow storm*
Patrick and the fox	*The catch*	*William and the spell*	*The secret cave*
Danger at sea	*William and the ghost*	*Space adventure*	*The island*
Karen's adventure	*William and the mouse*	*Monkey business*	*The chimney sweep*

Jackdaws

Please read the general introductory sections of this guide before starting on this section.

What are Jackdaws?

Jackdaws and *More Jackdaws* cover Stages 8–11 of the *Oxford Reading Tree*. They are written for competent independent readers with a mature interest level who need enjoyable reading material that will challenge and develop their reading skills further.

The components for the *Jackdaws* are:
- ◆ Ten *Jackdaws* anthologies
- ◆ Ten *More Jackdaws* anthologies
- ◆ Ten *Jackdaws Poetry* anthologies
- ◆ Ten *More Jackdaws Poetry* anthologies

There are also two *Jackdaws Reading and Spelling Tests*.

The Jackdaws anthologies

Stage 8   *The spoilt holiday*
          Anna's eggs
Stage 9   *Patrick and the fox*
          Danger at sea
Stage 10 *Karen's adventure*
          Kate's garden
Stage 11 *In the snow*
          The catch
          William and the ghost
          William and the mouse

The More Jackdaws anthologies

Stage 8   *The school play*
          The jokers
Stage 9   *William and the spell*
          Space adventure
Stage 10 *Monkey business*
          The playroom
Stage 11 *The snow storm*
          The secret cave
          The island
          The chimney sweep

Each of the *Jackdaws* anthologies contains one or more new stories, a section of non-fiction, and one or more traditional stories. There is a thematic link in each book and themes include: foxes; horses; races; dragons; mice; seeds and flowers; snow and ice; eggs and hatching; the sea; and ghosts. A number of different artists worked on the stories and illustrations are in a variety of styles, chosen to complement the different styles of writing.

The charts on pages 142 and 143 give details of the content of the *Jackdaws* and *More Jackdaws* anthologies.

The Jackdaws Poetry anthologies

Stage 8   *Horse poems*
          Egg poems
Stage 9   *Fox poems*
          Sea poems
Stage 10 *Dragon poems*
          Seed poems
Stage 11 *Snow poems*
          Sports poems
          Ghost poems
          Mouse poems

The More Jackdaws Poetry anthologies

Stage 8   *Giant poems*
          Twins poems
Stage 9   *Wizards poems*
          Space poems
Stage 10 *Monkey poems*
          Castle poems
Stage 11 *Star poems*
          Pirate poems
          Monster poems
          Night poems

How do the Jackdaws work?

The branch has several aims. First, and most important, is to give the good readers in the class a demanding but enjoyable read. Second, to encourage the readers to look beyond the parameters of the *Oxford Reading Tree*, by forming their own preferences and selecting other good stories to read. Third, to stimulate lively discussion about both the content of stories and the way in which stories are told.

Using the anthologies

The books should be introduced to the children using the five-step approach (see also 'Putting the *Oxford Reading Tree* approach into practice', page 17).

The five-step approach

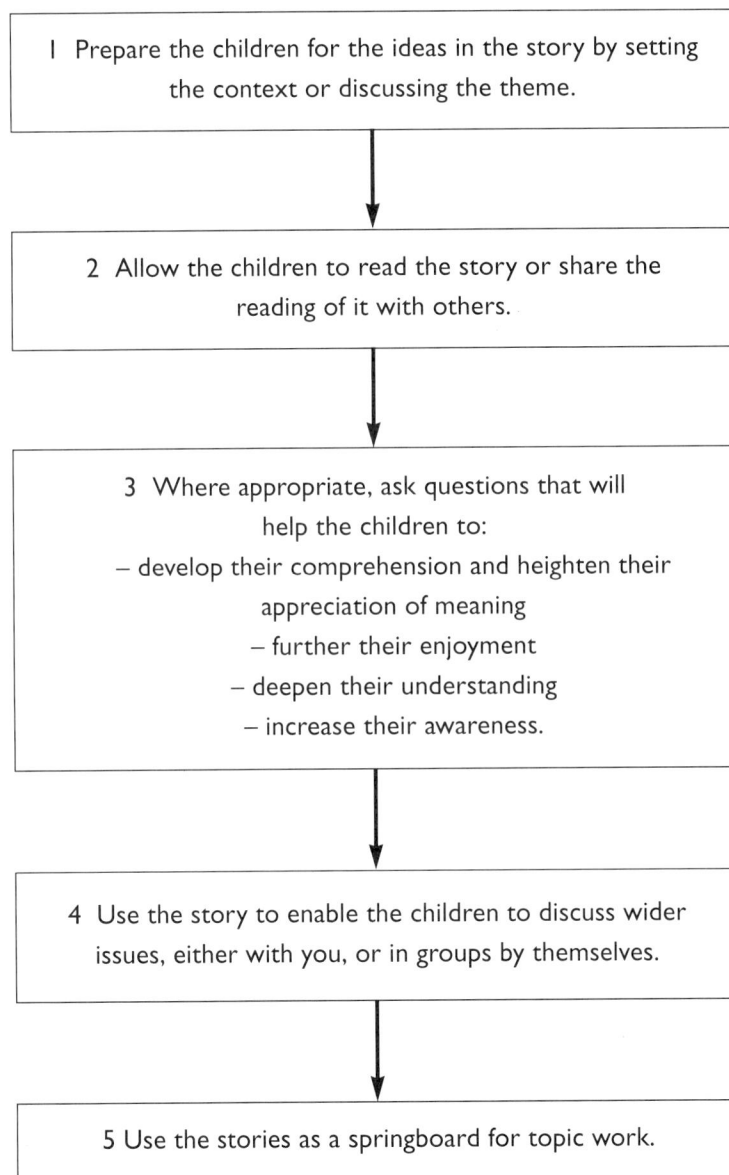

| 1 Prepare the children for the ideas in the story by setting the context or discussing the theme. |

↓

| 2 Allow the children to read the story or share the reading of it with others. |

↓

| 3 Where appropriate, ask questions that will help the children to:
– develop their comprehension and heighten their appreciation of meaning
– further their enjoyment
– deepen their understanding
– increase their awareness. |

↓

| 4 Use the story to enable the children to discuss wider issues, either with you, or in groups by themselves. |

↓

| 5 Use the stories as a springboard for topic work. |

Using the poetry books

The poetry books relate to the themes of the anthologies. They are colourfully illustrated by a variety of artists. They can be read alongside the anthologies or separately and provide ideal starting points for cross-curricular work.

Using the discussion questions

Each of the *Jackdaws* and *More Jackdaws* is accompanied by a selection of questions. Questions for discussion before reading the story introduce ideas and themes contained in the story. Questions for discussion after reading the story arouse general discussion and require children to think about the story, look for evidence and express an opinion. Children should be encouraged to read the non-fiction sections and formulate areas to research based on the element they find most interesting.

These questions have been arranged in order of the Stages – for example, questions for all the Stage 11 anthologies, whether *Jackdaws* or *More Jackdaws*, can be found together.

Using the language activities

There are three photocopiable language activity sheets for each anthology, starting on page 156. These have been arranged in the same way as the discussion questions, with all activities for a particular Stage being grouped together. They are provided as suggestions for you to choose from and adapt to suit the needs and attainments of your particular children.

The activity sheets are designed to sharpen children's awareness of text, and to develop reference and writing skills. They provide a range of lively and informal activities concentrating on the core skills of comprehension, grammar and punctuation.

The activities cover many aspects of the National Curriculum in England and Wales and the Scottish Office Guidelines, English Language 5–14. For grids showing specific skills/activities provided by the language activities please see page 155.

A detailed examination of some of the questions from the language activity sheets for *The chimney sweep* (*More Jackdaws* Stage 11) demonstrates how many of them can be useful for establishing quickly whether a child has read accurately and with understanding. Multiple choice questions are particularly helpful in assessing a child who may find writing more demanding than reading.

Page 213

1 Mr Webster treated Jake

kindly   badly   sensibly   fairly

The child who circles the word 'badly' has read accurately.

2 Slim was Jake's

friend   helper   dog   enemy

The child who selects 'enemy' has understood the relationship that exists between the main characters and is ready to express a positive opinion about them.

4 Webster spoke pleasantly to the housemaid because he was

hungry   kind   greedy
tired   polite

To reach the answer 'greedy' the reader has to employ complex reasoning. From the evidence so far we can deduce that Mr Webster does not treat people kindly. We can therefore infer, reason or predict that he is unlikely to change his character when faced with a servant, therefore he is unlikely to be 'polite' or 'kind'. He is unlikely to be 'hungry' because he has just eaten a huge meal. He is unlikely to be 'tired' because he has ridden in the cart. This process of elimination leads to 'greedy'. This answer also fits into our overall view of Mr Webster – one that is reinforced by his subsequent behaviour.

5 The word urchin is used on page 1. An urchin is a
poor boy   friendly dog
cruel man   rich boy

Urchin may be an unfamiliar word but its meaning can be deduced initially by using a syntactic strategy. The word itself is preceded by the adjective 'little'. There is pictorial evidence that suggests this refers to Jake. The word order and sentence structure seems to mean the word must be referring to the boy. The fact that Jake is a 'poor boy' is gained from a contextual strategy – the description of Jake's dressing conveys poverty. Using both strategies gives the answer 'poor boy'.

7 On page 6 Mr Webster gasped. On page 15 Jake gasped. When they gasped they were both
angry   frightened   amazed
worried   shocked

'Gasped' has to be read in the context of two different characters on two different occasions. 'Amazed' is the only possible answer for Mr Webster's response to the sight of so many chimneys. A careful reading of the text will reveal that Jake did not expect to see Scruff in the house. That meant he too was 'amazed'.

9 Jake had dreamt about being a chimney sweep because

it was his job
he had seen a painting
he had seen a television programme
he had found a secret passage

Choosing 'he had seen a painting' shows an understanding of a main theme – that the adventures experienced by Jake were only a dream.

Page 214

1 Number these instructions in the correct order for a servant about to make a fire...

The ability to list events in the correct order is a useful way of demonstrating how the main points of a passage – in this case a non-fiction text – have been understood.

2 If you had to live in Victorian times which of these jobs would you choose to do? ... Imagine you are living in Victorian times ...

Longer written answers allow readers to reveal the extent of their understanding. Some readers may try to answer such questions with a minimum of writing but should be encouraged to explore and express their understanding through a more detailed answer. Provided they restrict themselves to relevant remarks they may be seen to be moving towards embracing some of the elements of the higher level descriptions in the National Curriculum.

The Jackdaws Reading and Spelling Tests

Whilst there are no conventional *Oxford Reading Tree* workbooks to accompany the *Jackdaws* and *More Jackdaws* there are two *Jackdaws Reading and Spelling Tests* designed to practise and assess silent reading and spelling skills. They are designed to:

- help you to monitor and assess reading comprehension in order to plan effective future activities and teaching

- give pupils experience of working from more than one source at a time (their reading books and separate answer books)
- give pupils experience of the kind of tasks contained in reading comprehension and spelling tests designed for younger readers such as the Key Stage 1 tests in England and Wales and similar tests (and proposed tests in Scotland, Northern Ireland and the Irish Republic).

Record keeping

Page 223 provides a checklist of all the *Jackdaws* and *More Jackdaws* storybooks. At this stage, you may want to encourage the children to complete these themselves, so that they can record their own progress.

Assessment

There are four passages provided for *Jackdaws* and *More Jackdaws*. These are each about 100 words long and are designed to enable teachers to keep a running record when children are reading aloud. These passages may be found on pages 224–227. They are taken from:

Stage 8 *Anna's eggs* (pages 12–13)
Stage 9 *William and the spell* (pages 8–9)
Stage 10 *Karen's adventure* (page 17)
Stage 11 *The island* (page 12)

Each sheet has questions to assess the child's understanding of the text and ability to predict or remember what happened next.

Notes on calculating an accuracy rate are on page 27.

Book review

There is a book review sheet at the end of this section which can be completed after reading any book. It is a useful way of encouraging children to reflect on a book and can reveal a depth of understanding and enjoyment. However, children should not be forced to review every book they read.

Stage	Jackdaws title	Theme	Titles of stories	Range of stories
8	*The spoilt holiday*	Horses	The spoilt holiday All about horses The most famous horse in the world	Modern fiction Non-fiction Myth/Legend
8	*Anna's eggs*	Eggs and hatching	Anna's eggs All about eggs The ugly duckling	Modern fiction Non-fiction Traditional story
9	*Patrick and the fox*	Foxes	Patrick and the fox All about foxes A kindness rewarded	Modern fiction Non-fiction Traditional story
9	*Danger at sea*	Sea	Danger at sea All about lighthouses Grace Darling	Modern fiction Non-fiction Biography
10	*Karen's adventure*	Dragons	Karen's adventure All about dragons Hott's first dragon	Modern fiction Non-fiction Myth/Legend
10	*Kate's garden*	Seeds and flowers	Kate's garden All about seeds The wise chicken The gift of corn	Modern fiction Non-fiction Traditional story Traditional story

11	*In the snow*	Snow and ice	William in the snow
			All about snow and ice
			The bear's tail
			Why the bear sleeps
			   through the winter
			How the chipmunk
			   got his stripes
				Modern fiction
				Non-fiction
				Myth/Legend
				Myth/Legend
				
				Myth/Legend

11	*The catch*	Races	The catch Chinese horoscopes The race	Modern fiction Non-fiction Myth/Legend
11	*William and the ghost*	Ghosts	William and the ghost All about ghosts Miss Terry's holiday	Modern fiction Non-fiction Traditional story
11	*William and the mouse*	Mice	William and the mouse All about mice Yin Ling's tale The mouse's marriage	Modern fiction Non-fiction Modern fiction Traditional story

Stage	More Jackdaws title	Theme	Titles of stories	Range of stories
8	*The school play*	Giants	The school play Why do we tell stories about giants? A real giant The giant baby	Modern fiction Non-fiction Non-fiction Traditional story
8	*The jokers*	Twins	The jokers Stories about twins The Emperor's lesson	Modern fiction Myth/Legend Traditional story
9	*William and the spell*	Wizards	William and the spell Wizards The wizard's day off	Modern fiction Non-fiction Traditional story
9	*Space adventure*	Space	The space adventure Space Planets The little girl who wanted the stars	Modern fiction Non-fiction Non-fiction Traditional story
10	*Monkey business*	Monkeys	Monkey business A chimp for the day Chimpanzees Monkeys Leave it until tomorrow The monkey and the shark The stone monkey	Modern fiction Modern fiction Non-fiction Non-fiction Myth/Legend Traditional story Myth/Legend
10	*The playroom*	Castles	The playroom Castles The ghostly battle	Modern fiction Non-fiction Myth/Legend
11	*The snow storm*	Stars	The snow storm Stars The star child	Modern fiction Non-fiction Traditional story
11	*The secret cave*	Pirates	The secret cave Smugglers The phantom ship	Modern fiction Non-fiction Traditional story
11	*The island*	Monsters	The island Monsters in the water! Mermaids A strange island The water horse	Modern fiction Non-fiction Myth/Legend Traditional story Traditional story
11	*The chimney sweep*	Night	The chimney sweep Living in the past Hans Andersen The little match girl	Modern fiction Non-fiction Biography Traditional story

Discussion questions

The spoilt holiday (Jackdaws)

The spoilt holiday

Before reading the story

Have you ever really looked forward to something like going to the swimming pool or going to stay with your best friend, and then not been able or allowed to go? How did you feel? What does 'disappointed' mean? What do you like about horses? Have you ever ridden a horse? What does it feel like?

Have you ever been to a fairground? Have you ever seen a roundabout with horses? This is the story of a little girl who loved horses and was looking forward to spending her summer holiday riding.

Do you know any old people? What do you do to look after them?

After reading the story

Do you think Lucy's holiday was spoilt after all? Why not?

Do you think Mum knew that the horse was magic? How do you know?

What was in the big parcel? Would you like to have a magic horse?

Lucy went to India to watch tigers, and to the North Pole to look at the polar bears. If you had a magic horse, where would you like to go?

The most famous horse in the world

Before reading the story

Why do horses have to be tamed? What would happen if you tried to ride an untamed horse?

When a horse lets a rider get on his back he needs to be sure the rider won't hurt him, and the rider needs to be sure the horse won't throw him off. What is the word we use to describe this feeling? Can you think of any people we trust?

After reading the story

What was frightening the horse?

Why did Alexander tell the man to turn the horse around? What is a shadow?

When Alex grew up he became a famous King and was called Alexander the Great. What do you know about Alexander the Great?

Anna's eggs (Jackdaws)

Anna's eggs

Before reading the story

Are you a messy person? Have you ever been in trouble for making a mess? What happened?

Do you have a pet? Which animals are good to keep as pets? Why? Would chickens make good pets? Why do some people keep chickens?

What is an incubator? Have you ever seen an egg hatching? This story is about hatching.

After reading the story

Why did Auntie Jo leave Anna in charge of the incubator, do you think? Was it because she had to go out or do you think she knew what was going to happen?

Why do you think the eggs had to be turned? How did the little crosses on the eggs help?

If Anna bought some eggs from the shop and tried to hatch them they would not turn into chickens. Do you know why? (You can avoid this question if you think the children are not ready for a basic biology lesson.)

The ugly duckling

Before reading the story

Have you ever been left out of something? How would you feel if you were not invited to a party you wanted to go to? Or if you were left out of a game you wanted to play?

Do you know why some birds fly south for winter? Some animals and birds change as they grow up. They change in size, colour and sometimes shape. What does a tadpole grow into? What happens to a caterpillar? What does a duckling look like when it first hatches?

After reading the story
Was the ugly duckling really ugly, or was he just different from the other ducklings?
Why couldn't the ugly duckling make friends with the cat and the hen? Did they like the same things?
Is this story just a story? Do you think this story teaches us anything? Shouldn't the other animals have treated the ugly duckling with more kindness?
The ugly duckling was really a cygnet. How do you think he felt when he turned into a swan?

The school play (More Jackdaws)

The school play

Before reading the story
Do you perform plays at your school? When do you perform these plays? If you were allowed to choose any story to turn into a school play, which story would you choose?
What do you prefer – reading a story to yourself, having a story read to you, watching a film or seeing a play performed by live actors?

After reading the story
If Father O'Leary hadn't been injured Ben wouldn't have been in the play. Can you think of a part Ben could have played in his wheelchair? Do you think Ben could have been the cow, or the man who buys the cow with the magic beans?
The village school used a ladder for their beanstalk. How would you design a beanstalk that twisted like a real beanstalk, but up which actors could climb?

The giant baby

Before reading the story
People used to make up stories about giants to explain things nobody could understand. Nowadays people make up stories about creatures from outer space (aliens!) to explain things they can't understand. Do you believe there are other life forms in the universe?

After reading the story
The giants in this story are very strong but they are not very bright. Oonagh is small but clever. Which would you choose to be – big and strong, or small and clever? Why?

The jokers (More Jackdaws)

The jokers

Before reading the story
If you play a trick on someone and it is successful you may find it very funny. The person who has been tricked may not be so happy! Have you ever played a successful trick on anyone? Has anyone ever played a trick on you that has made you cross?
Have you ever disguised yourself? Have you ever pretended to be someone – or something – else? How do you think you could make yourself look like one of your friends?

After reading the story
Are you a twin? Would you like to be a twin? Would it be fun looking like someone else? Could you really play tricks like Alex and Tog? Or do you think you might find it annoying – especially if people didn't treat you like an individual?
Why does Uncle Brian say: 'If people didn't eat their dinners, farmers like me would be out of a job'?. What does he mean?

The Emperor's lesson

Before reading the story
Do you think it would be better to be a rich king with no friends, or a poor farmer with many friends? Why do you think like this?
What do you think is the most important thing the ruler of a country should try to do?

After reading the story
What do you think the double was? Was it a ghost? Was it part of a dream? Was it real?
What was the only way the Emperor's subjects could recognize their ruler? How do you recognize people?

Stage 9

Patrick and the fox (Jackdaws)

Patrick and the fox

Before reading the story

Have you ever seen a hunt? What does it look like? Who takes part? What do they do?
Some animals are pests. Can you think of any? Why do some farmers think foxes can do harm? Can you think of any animals which are pests?

After reading the story

What knocked the dustbin over?
Why didn't Patrick tell anyone about the fox?
Why does Patrick think it's wrong to chase foxes?

A kindness rewarded

Before reading the story

What does 'to do someone a good turn' mean? Have you ever helped someone or done someone a good turn? Has anyone ever helped you?
Do you know someone who makes your wishes come true? If you really want something, who is the person who usually gets it for you?
Foxes are sometimes described as crafty. Why do you think this is so?

After reading the story

Do you think the young man deserved to marry the princess? Why?
Why is the story called 'A kindness rewarded'? Who was kind and who was rewarded?

Danger at sea (Jackdaws)

Danger at sea

Before reading the story

Have you ever been to the seaside? What sort of things did you do?
The seaside can be a dangerous place. What dangers can you think of at the seaside? What dangers can you think of in towns, in the country?
What things warn people of dangers? Can you think of

some warnings? (Examples might be a burglar alarm, a flare, a red traffic light, a flag.)
What colour usually means danger? What colour usually means it is safe?

After reading the story

What do we learn from this story? Why is it important to obey warnings?
What things should you do to stay safe at the seaside?
Why was Mike swept out to sea? What is a current? What is a tide?
The inshore rescue boat saved Mike from drowning. Which emergency service should you call if:
- there is a fire?
- there is an accident?
- there is a burglary?
- there is a cat caught in a tree?

How do you call an emergency service?
Why is it a good thing to know how to swim?

Grace Darling

Before reading the story

What is a hero or heroine? Can you think of any stories about heroism?
There are many stories about people who save other people's lives. This story is about a young girl who became famous because she saved nine people's lives. Can you think of any famous women who were brave and saved other people's lives?

After reading the story

What kind of girl was Grace? Can you think of any words to describe her?
How do you think the people felt when they were clinging to the rocks in the sea? How do you think they felt when they were safely back in the lighthouse? What should you do when people are in shock?

William and the spell (More Jackdaws)

William and the spell

Before reading the story

The characters in this story are affected a great deal by a story in a book that they find in the library, and by the television. If you had to choose between having a shelf of books from the library and a television set, which would you choose?

One of the main characters in the book William finds in the library is a wizard. The wizard makes a spell to do with television. If you could make a spell to do with television, what would it be?

After reading the story

Why does William's mum turn off the television?

Why does William's mum take him to the library?

How can you tell that William's mum was pleased when he asked her about how the story should end?

How would you make the story about Gary end?

The wizard's day off

Before reading the story

Do you know the names of any wizards who appear in other stories? Do you know any stories where a magic spell changes the lives of the characters?

One of the characters in this story, Hans, is learning to be a wizard. What would be the first piece of magic that you would want to learn?

After reading the story

Why do you think Hans was only allowed to practise when the Wizard was at home?

Why do you think Hans wasn't allowed to use magic when he was doing all the housework?

Why didn't Hans get the housework done on time?

Why do you think spells are often made to rhyme?

Why do you think the Wizard didn't use magic to clear up the mess?

Space adventure (More Jackdaws)

Space adventure

Before reading the story

What sort of alien creatures would you like to meet?

On what sort of planet would you like them to live?

If visitors came to Earth from another planet what do you think they might want from us? Do you think they would be friendly? How do you think they would travel through space?

After reading the story

Why do William and Hamid choose to go on the

Space Ride at the fair?

Why do you think the little green men laughed at William and Hamid?

What do you think would have happened if William and Hamid had taken another ride?

The little girl who wanted the stars

Before reading the story

Have you ever wanted something badly, only to be told that it is impossible? What did you feel like when you were told this? Did it stop you wishing you could have what you wanted so badly?

Have you ever succeeded in doing something that most people thought you would never do? What did it feel like when you succeeded?

After reading the story

Do you think the girl was brave to set out to look for the stars, or do you think she was silly?

Why couldn't the girl catch the stars in the pond?

What was the riddle the fairies gave the little girl? What was the answer to the riddle?

Why did the light get brighter at the top of the stairs?

Do you think the girl would try to reach the stars again?

Stage 10

Karen's adventure (Jackdaws)

Karen's adventure

Before reading the story

What type of adventure would you like to have?

Have you ever had a secret, something you didn't want to tell grown-ups about? How did you feel?

Have you ever looked after a baby animal? What did you do? What would you do if you had to look after a baby dragon?

Can you think of any animals who are pretty and friendly when they are small but who become dangerous when they grow up?

After reading the story

Do you think Karen should have climbed the tree to get over the wall? Why was this dangerous?

Why do you think Gran's grandfather locked the door and told Gran not to go into that part of the garden?

Why did Karen decide to keep the dragon a secret? Do you think she was right? Why?

What happened to the dragon in the kitchen? How did it change? Why do you think this happened?

What did the warning mean 'He's afraid of mirrors. Don't feed him chicken'?

In the story the warning was disobeyed. Do you think this was Karen's fault? Why not?

What is a reflection? What happened when the dragon saw his reflection in the mirror? Why did Karen decide to show the dragon the mirror?

Do you think the dragon was a kind or nasty dragon? Why?

At the end of the story how do you think Karen felt about the dragon? What words would you use to describe Karen in this story e.g. inquisitive, brave, kind?

Hott's first dragon

Before reading the story

Have you ever been afraid of something? Do you know any bullies? What do bullies do?

Why is it wrong to laugh at someone because they can't do something? What should you do instead?

After reading the story

Why do you think it took a long time for the King's letter to reach Bothva? How long does a letter take today?

Why did Bothva walk to Denmark? It must have been a long journey. How would he travel today?

Why do you think the King had gone hunting instead of waiting to welcome Bothva when he arrived?

Do you think Hott was a coward? Why?

What does 'to sit at the King's right hand' mean? Do you have any special places in the classroom, e.g. a birthday chair?

How did Hott become brave?

Why do you think Bothva pretended that Hott killed the dragon?

What do we learn from this story?

Kate's garden (Jackdaws)

Kate's garden

Before reading the story

Have you ever planted anything and watched it grow? What did you plant? Did you plant seeds or plants?

Can you think of any little animals who like to eat plants?

What happens to a seed when it is planted?

After reading the story

Who played the tricks on Jo? How do you know? Is it possible to grow sweets? Do you think Jo believed she had grown sweets?

Why did Mum tell the girls to dig out all the weeds, dig up the soil and take out any big stones?

Why did Mum tell the girls to plant their seeds in seedboxes and not plant them straight in the garden?

Why did the seeds in the seedboxes not grow?

Why did Jo's lettuces not grow?

What is a compost heap? Why did Jo throw the lettuces on to the compost heap?

The wise chicken

Before reading the story

Can you think of any crops?

What crops are used to make bread?

What is bread made from? One of the most important ingredients in bread is flour. Do you know how flour is made? This story tells us about how a chicken once cut the wheat, made some flour and baked bread.

After reading the story

Why did the chicken decide not to eat the grains of wheat? What did she decide to do with them instead? What does this story tell us about helping others? Why didn't the chicken share her bread with the other animals? Do you think she was right to do this? What does 'selfish' mean? Why shouldn't you be selfish? What things should you share with your friends?

The gift of corn

Before reading the story

Why do birds fly away in winter? Is it because it is too cold and there is nothing to eat? This story tells us what happened one winter when it was so cold people couldn't hunt or fish and had nothing to eat. What is corn on the cob? Have you ever eaten it? What does it look like?

After reading the story

Before the people learned how to grow corn what did they eat? Why did the Chief tell his people to go away? What sort of a Chief was he? Who do you think Red Feather really was? How do you know? Why was he called Red Feather? What did the discovery of corn mean to the tribe? Why were the tribe never hungry again? Can you think of ways we store food nowadays so that we can eat it at any time of the year? e.g. tin strawberries, freeze vegetables.

Monkey business (More Jackdaws)

Monkey business

Before reading the story

Why do people keep wild animals in zoos? Have you visited a zoo? Did you think the zoo was doing a good job? Was it looking after the animals well? If you were a wild animal would you like to be kept in a zoo? What is your favourite animal? Would you like to have your favourite animal as a pet? Could you keep it in the place you live at the moment? What would you have to do to look after it? What would it eat? Where would it sleep? If you had to become an animal for a day, which animal

would you choose to be? Why would you want to be that animal? How would your life be different?

After reading the story

Do you think Mr Jolly was a good zoo keeper? Why do you think like this? If you were an animal would you like Mr Jolly to look after you? Does Mr Jolly have any pets of his own? What are they? Where do they live?

The stone monkey

Before reading the story

Have you ever seen a film or a television programme with a monkey or an ape as its star? What happened? What can a monkey do that you would like to do? When would being like a monkey be useful to you?

After reading the story

What were the five pillars at the edge of the world? What do you think this story is supposed to teach us? Where do you think the stone egg could have come from? Do you think it would be useful to be made of stone or do you think it might be a problem?

The playroom (More Jackdaws)

The playroom

Before reading the story

Do you have a favourite toy? Why do you like it? Would you swap it for another toy? Have you ever seen the sort of toys your parents, or even your grandparents, or your great-grandparents, used to play with? Could you play with those toys? When you play with toys do you make them come to life? Do you give them different voices? Do you make them speak out loud? Do you give them exciting adventures?

After reading the story

Do you think Jo really rescued her great-grandfather, or do you think it was only a dream? Which of the other toys do you think Jo could have used to help in the escape? How would she have used it?

The ghostly battle

Before reading the story
This story is set in the days of the famous King Arthur. Do you know the names of any of the knights who served this famous king?
In this story a living man fights a ghost. Who do you think will win? What do you think would happen if you challenged a ghost to a running race?

After reading the story
What makes you think the rider might not be a ghost?
What makes you think the rider must be a ghost?
Do you think the horse was a ghost? Why do you think this way?
If the rider was a ghost why do you think he haunted the old fort at the top of Wandlebury Hill?

Stage 11

In the snow (Jackdaws)

William in the snow

Before reading the story

When do we usually have snow? What things do you like about snow? What things don't you like? What games do you play in the snow? What clothes do you wear in the snow?

What is ice? Why can it be dangerous?

After reading the story

How did William feel when he looked out of the window and saw the snow? How do you feel when you see the snow?

Do you remember another story about these two bullies, Toby Keene and Jim Bowman?★ What happened? Do you think Toby and Jim had learned a lesson?

Why is it dangerous to walk on ice?

What do you think happened to Toby and Jim?

★ *The emergency* (Robins Stage 8)

The bear's tail

Before reading the story

Where do polar bears live? What does a polar bear look like? This is the story of the polar bear who has a short stumpy tail.

After reading the story

Where did the fox get the fish?

Do you think he was right to play a trick on the polar bear?

How did the bear feel when he saw the hunter coming towards him?

Can you think of any other animals who have short stumpy tails? (e.g. Manx cats)

Why the bear sleeps through the winter

Before reading the story

In winter it is difficult for animals to find food. What do birds do, where do they go, in winter? Some animals sleep throughout winter. What is the word we use to describe this? Can you think of any animals who hibernate? What do they do for food?

After reading the story

What is a good turn?

Why were the horse and the reindeer unkind to the old man? What word would you use to describe them?

Why did the bear help the old man? What word would you use to describe him?

Why is it important to help old people? Can you think of any ways in which you could help an old person?

How was the bear rewarded for his kindness?

The catch (Jackdaws)

The catch

Before reading the story

What happened on open day?

What games do you play on sports day? Can you think of some funny races (e.g. egg and spoon race, 3-legged race) as well as some serious races?

How do you play rounders?

How would you feel if you wanted to take part in sports but weren't able to?

After reading the story

What would you feel like if your legs wouldn't work? What things could you do and what things couldn't you do?

Why couldn't Ben do sports?

What do we learn from this story about how disabled people feel and about how we should treat them?

The race

Before reading the story

What twelve animals rule the Chinese years?

Do you know why the Chinese call each year after one of the twelve animals? This story tells you why.

After reading the story

How did the Jade Emperor show himself to be a wise ruler?

Why did the Jade Emperor not choose the winning animal to rule over the others?

Do we learn anything about how animals and people behave in this story?

William and the ghost (*Jackdaws*)

William and the ghost

Before reading the story
What is a ghost? Have you ever seen one? There are no such things as ghosts but people like to tell stories about them. Why do you think that is? What ghost stories do you know?

Ghosts are said to haunt some places or buildings. What does to 'haunt' mean? What types of places are said to have ghosts?

Have you ever visited a haunted castle? This is the story about what happened when William and Hamid went on a school trip to a haunted castle.

After reading the story
Do you think William really saw the old Earl? How do you know?

Have you ever had a dream which you thought was real? What was it about? What happened?

Have you ever visited an old castle? What things did you see?

Miss Terry's holiday

Before reading the story
There are many stories about strange happenings: fairy tales and ghost stories. What is the difference between a ghost and a fairy? A ghost is supposed to be the spirit of a person who really existed a long time ago. This story is about a teacher who was helped by the ghost of a little girl.

Imagine you went back in time to when your grand-parents were children. What would be different about the house where they lived and your house? What about lighting, heating?

After reading the story
How did Miss Terry know the little girl was a ghost? In the story we are given a hint that something strange was going to happen. Where was that?

Why do you think it was difficult for Miss Terry to believe that she had seen a ghost?

Do you think the little girl really didn't know what a telephone was? Why?

Why were there no modern things in the kitchen of the cottage?

What was different about the cottage when Miss Terry went back to it?

William and the mouse (*Jackdaws*)

William and the mouse

Before reading the story
Have you ever had a pet mouse? Did he ever escape from his cage? What happened?

What things do you have to do to look after a pet mouse properly?

Have you ever done something at home that you were not supposed to do? What happened?

After reading the story
Why did William think that if he put some cheese in the middle of the floor he would catch Eenor?

Why did the boys not find Eenor even though they looked in all the furniture?

Why do you think Julie didn't say anything about the room being in a mess?

What do you think happened to William when Mum saw the mess?

Yin Ling's tale

Before reading the story
What do you think it feels like to be a mouse? What would you eat? Where would you sleep?

Why do people try to get rid of mice? What things do they use to get rid of mice?

What household animal are mice most afraid of? Why?

After reading the story
Do you think Yin Ling really became a mouse, or was she only dreaming? How do you know?

What makes you think that something did happen during the night?

The mouse's marriage

Before reading the story
What do you think is the strongest thing in all the world? Why?

In some countries parents decide who their children will marry. Can you think of the good things about this, and the bad things?

Have you ever been to a wedding? Who was getting married? What happened?

After reading the story
Why did Mr Mouse want his daughter to marry the strongest person on earth?
Why is everyone happy at the end of the story?
What do we learn from this story?

The snow storm (More Jackdaws)

The snow storm

Before reading the story
This story takes place in bad weather. A snow storm isn't the only sort of bad weather. How many other types of bad weather can you think of? Have you ever been trapped inside by bad weather? What was it like? Were you frightened or was it exciting?
To cheer up the children who are trapped one of the older characters in the book reads them a story. If you were cut off in a lonely cottage which book would you like to have with you? Why would you choose this book?

After reading the story
Do you think Rob and Becky's dad was sensible to set off in such bad weather? Did he have to go out? What else could he have done?
The children were safe in the cottage. What made them leave the cottage and go out into the snow? What would you have done?
Why was the little fir tree luckier than the bigger trees?

The star child

Before reading the story
Stars are some of the most mysterious things in the universe. They are millions of miles away but we can see them without leaving our homes. For thousands of years people have thought that the stars make shapes in the night sky. Do you know the names of any of these shapes?

After reading the story
Do you think the woodcutter should have told the boy that he found him? What would the boy have been like if he had thought the woodcutter and his wife were his real parents?
Why was the boy surprised when the beggars said they

were his parents? Why did he expect to be the son of special people?
Why had the boy fallen to earth?
Do you think the woodcutter had seen a falling star on the night he found the boy? If it wasn't a star, what do you think made the light?
What do you think this story is trying to teach us?

The secret cave (More Jackdaws)

The secret cave

Before reading the story
Have you been in a cave? Have you been underground? Have you ever been anywhere where there was no light at all?
If you were exploring a cave what important things would you take with you?

After reading the story
Do you think Hamid and William really had an adventure, or was it just a game they were playing? Can you explain why you think this way? What clues are there in the story that helped you make your mind up?
At the end of the story Hamid and William discover that Captain Hood isn't a sea captain at all. If you read page 2 again you might be able to find a mistake that Captain Hood makes about food and drink that proves he knows nothing at all about the sea. What does Captain Hood say that is wrong?

The phantom ship

Before reading the story
Have you read any sea stories? You may have heard of the journeys of Jason and the Argonauts and Odysseus, or of the pirates in *Treasure Island*. What sort of adventures do you expect to hear about in a sea story?

After reading the story
How could Ben tell that there was someone with Captain Grimes?
How many times did Ben see the Dutchman? Where did he see him?
How did Captain Grimes make his money?
When should Captain Grimes have become suspicious of the merchant ship?
Why did the Dutchman sink The Sea Lion?

The island (*More Jackdaws*)

The island

Before reading the story

In this story a man wants to build a Monster Theme Park in a beautiful part of Scotland. Do you like the idea of going to a theme park? Do you like the idea of spending time in a quiet part of the countryside? How would you feel if someone said they were going to build a theme park near your house?

Another part of the same story tells about a monster that is supposed to have lived for hundreds of years in an old ruined castle. Do you know any stories about monsters? Have you heard about Bigfoot, the Abominable Snowman or the Loch Ness monster?

After reading the story

Do you think any of the characters in the story have seen any more of the monster than a thin, green arm? If you do, who are these characters, and why do you think they have seen the monster?

If there was a monster living in the ruined castle do you think it would like to have a theme park named after it? What do you think the monster would do if hundreds of tourists came to see it?

The water horse

Before reading the story

This story is set in Scotland too. Why do you think so many stories about monsters are set in lonely places where few people live?

If you lived in Roman times and were transported forward in time to experience modern life, what do you think you might believe were monsters?

Monsters in stories can often change their shapes. What shape would you like to take?

After reading the story

What is the first clue Janet discovers that makes her think her visitor is the water horse?

What is the only thing that can stop the water horse?

Why do you think the water horse wants the land?

The chimney sweep (*More Jackdaws*)

The chimney sweep

Before reading the story

Have you ever seen a chimney being swept? What sort of equipment do you think chimney sweeps need to do their jobs?

This story is set in Victorian times when many children in Britain didn't go to school but went out to work instead. What sort of jobs do children do nowadays? Would you like to leave school and go out to work instead?

The story takes place in a huge Victorian house that needs a great many servants to look after it. What has taken the place of those servants?

After reading the story

Who is Jake's only friend?

Where did Jake go to sleep?

Where is Jake when he wakes up?

Would you have liked to have been a child in Victorian times? Why do you feel this way?

The little match girl

Before reading the story

This story is set on New Year's Eve. Do you celebrate the New Year? What do you think people are looking forward to in the New Year? Do you know what a New Year's Resolution is?

The little match girl is very poor and has no home to go to. She becomes very cold. When you become cold how do you try to keep warm? What do you think the little match girl might do?

The little match girl imagines her favourite meal. If you could choose any meal in the world, what would it be?

After reading the story

Why do you think no-one takes any notice of the little match girl?

At the end of the story the little match girl disappeared. Where do you think she went?

Why do you think Hans Andersen wrote this story? Do you think he was trying to teach his readers something? Was he trying to change the way people treated children?

Jackdaws and More Jackdaws language activities grid

	COMPREHENSION	SEQUENCING	IMAGINATIVE WRITING	NON-FICTION WRITING/ FEATURES	EXPRESSING PREFERENCES/ OPINIONS	VOCABULARY	PUNCTUATION	EXTENSION
Stage 8								
The spoilt holiday	p 156 p 157 p 158		p 158					
Anna's eggs	p 159 p 160 p 161	p 160				p 161		
The school play	p 162 p 164	p 162	p 163				p 163	
The jokers	p 165 p 166	p 165	p 167		p 165			
Stage 9								
Patrick and the fox	p 168 p 169 p 170		p 169	p 170				p 168
Danger at sea	p 172 p 173			p 173	p 172			p 171
William and the spell	p 174 p 176		p 175				p 176	
Space adventure	p 177 p 178 p 179				p 177 p 179			p 178
Stage 10								
Karen's adventure	p 180 p 182		p 181 p 182	p 180				
Kate's garden	p 183 p 184 p 185					p 184		p 183 p 185
Monkey business	p 186 p 187 p 188		p 187		p 188		p 186 p 187	
The playroom	p 189 p 190 p 191			p 191		p 191	p 190	
Stage 11								
In the snow	p 192 p 193 p 194		p 194	p 193				
The catch	p 195 p 196 p 197				p 196			p 197
William and the ghost	p 198 p 200	p 200	p 200	p 199				p 199
William and the mouse	p 201 p 202 p 203		p 203	p 202				p 201
The snow storm	P 204 p 206	p 205	p 205		p 204 p 206			
The secret cave	p 207 p 208 p 209		p 208		p 207 p 209			p 208
The island	p 210 p 211 p 212			p 211	p 212			p 211
The chimney sweep	p 213	p 214	p 214		p 214		p 215	

The spoilt holiday

Here are some descriptions of pages in the story. Write down the number of the page on which each picture appears. The first one has been done for you.

1   Lucy is carrying some books.

     This picture is on page eleven.

2   In this picture Lucy is eating breakfast.

     _____

3   Lucy is holding a toy pony in this picture.

     _____

4   In this picture it is raining.

     _____

5   There is a boat in this picture.

     _____

Here are some descriptions of things that happen in the story. Write down the number of the page where these things happen.

6   Mum sat down and looked at the road atlas on page _____.

7   Lucy unpacked her suitcase on page _____.

8   Lucy heard a creaking noise on page _____.

9   We find out where Uncle Walter got the horse on page _____.

All about horses

Write a sentence to answer each of these questions.

1   What was the main difference between the horses we see today and the horses that lived millions of years ago?

_____

_____

2   Why were horses very useful animals to have on farms?

_____

_____

3   Why do you think ponies were used in mines instead of horses?

_____

_____

4   Write down the names of two other animals that are in the same family as horses and ponies.

5   Artists have always liked drawing horses. Draw a picture of a horse taking part in a sport.

The most famous horse in the world

Draw a circle around the right word.

1   The horse wasn't shown to the King because it was too

               old   young   wild   quiet   weak

2   The horse kicked and reared because it was

               nasty   frightened   stupid   savage

3   The only person who could ride the horse was

               Philip   the groom   Alexander   Oxhead

Answer this question.

4   Why did Alexander tell the men to turn the horse around?

      _____

5   Write down a sentence from the story that shows you Alexander treated the horse gently.

      _____

6   You are a wild horse and you don't want anyone to ride you. One day you are taken to a farm where they train horses. Out of the corner of your eye you see the rider who is going to try and stay on your back.

Make a list of five tricks you will use to get rid of the rider. One has been written for you.

How to get rid of riders

1   Rear up.

2   _____

3   _____

4   _____

5   _____

Anna's eggs

Find the words and write them in the boxes.

Find a word on page 12 that describes this egg.

Find a word on page 8 that describes this egg.

Find a word on page 10 that describes what this chicken is doing.

Find two words on page 13 that you can use to fill in these two labels.

Read page 10.
Where should the cross be on Friday?

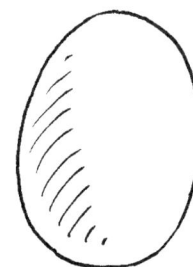

Monday

Friday

All about eggs

Answer these questions.

1   Why do some birds lay white eggs?

_____

2   Write these words in the correct box:

hummingbird egg   ostrich egg   bead   melon

BIG	SMALL

3   Draw a circle around the best word.

Eggs are

        square   round   oval   triangular

4   When a baby bird is still inside its egg it feeds on two different types of food. What are the names of those foods?

_____ and _____

5   Put these events in a cuckoo's life in the correct order. The first event has been numbered for you.

☐   The cuckoo chick throws the other eggs out of the nest.

☐   The birds who made the nest feed the cuckoo chick.

1   A cuckoo lays its egg in another bird's nest.

☐   The cuckoo chick hatches out of its egg.

☐   When it is fully grown the cuckoo flies away.

The ugly duckling

Write sentences to answer these questions.

1   What was unusual about the egg the ugly duckling came from?

_____

2   Why did the ugly duckling run away?

_____

_____

3   How did the old woman think the ugly duckling might be useful?

_____

_____

4   Why was it difficult for the ugly duckling to find food in the winter?

_____

_____

5   The proper name for a young swan is a cygnet. Draw lines to join these parents to
     their young. Use a dictionary if you are not sure which belongs to which.

swan	piglet
hen	calf
pig	cygnet
cow	chick
deer	cub
bear	fawn

The school play

Draw a circle around the word that you think gives the best answer.

1   The school play was going to take place in the

        morning   evening   afternoon   night

2   The tug-of-war was going to take place in the

        morning   evening   afternoon   night

3   When Ben first heard about the play he was

        excited   sad   worried   scared   angry

4   When Ben saw the scenery being made he was

        excited   sad   worried   scared   angry

5   A person who tells actors their lines if they forget them is a

        designer   teacher   author   director   prompter

6   Number these events in the right order. The first one has been done for you.

    [   ] Ben acts in the school play.

    [   ] Father O'Leary breaks his leg.

    [1] Jenny and Nazirah fall over.

    [   ] Ben sits on Mr Drury's shoulders.

    [   ] Father O'Leary trips over.

7   Ben and Mr Drury could be the giant in the play because:

Ben knew the giant's _____.

Mr Drury knew the giant's _____.

Why do we tell stories about giants?

Answer the questions.

1   The capital letters have been left out of these sentences. Write out the sentences putting them all in. Remember to use capital letters for the names of places and people as well as for the beginning of sentences.

this is silbury hill in wiltshire. it was used by the people who lived in this part of england. nobody knows why it was built so people made up stories to explain why it is there.

_____

_____

_____

_____

2   We know that the people who lived in Marlborough had made the giant angry, but we don't know how. Imagine you lived in Marlborough and that it was you who had made the giant angry! Here is a page from your diary. Finish it off.

Dear Diary,

Well, today started rather strangely. Mum gave me porridge for breakfast. I hate porridge so when she wasn't looking I picked up my bowl and threw it out of the window. That was a mistake.

_____

_____

_____

_____

The giant baby

Answer these questions.

1   What was worrying Finn at the beginning of the story?

_____

_____

2   The other giant went to Scotland and caused a great deal of damage. This is the
Wanted Poster that appeared in Scotland. Use the pictures and the story to fill
in the gaps.

Wanted

For destroying the forests of Scotland

This giant

Height _____

Hair colour_____

Clothing _____

Special features _____

The jokers

Draw a circle around the word that gives the best answer.

1   The name of Sue's brother is

Alex   Adam   Carla   Max   Tog

2   The name of Alex's brother is

Jet   Adam   Carla   Max   Tog

3   Number these events in the right order. The first one has been done for you.

☐   Alex tells Adam and Sue he is Tog's twin.

1   Adam and Sue meet Alex.

☐   Tog goes to the circus with Adam, Sue and Carla.

☐   Alex falls off the horse.

☐   Alex goes to the farm with Adam and Sue.

☐   Tog rides on the circus horse.

4   Answer these questions.

Why do you think the story is called 'The jokers'?

_____

_____

5   Who would you like to be in this story? Tick one name only.

Adam ☐   Sue ☐   Tog ☐   Carla ☐   Alex ☐

Why did you choose this character?

_____

_____

Stories about twins

Answer these questions.

1   Romulus and Remus were the names of two

         wolves   brothers   cities   friends   horses

2   Rome is named after

         Remus   Romulus   Mars   Castor   Pollux

3   The star sign of the twins is called

         Capricorn   Cancer   Virgo   Leo   Gemini

4   On page 22 and page 24 the writer uses a word that means an old story that has been told for hundreds of years and tells of unusual and amazing events.

     That word is

5   Here is Castor's birth certificate. Fill in the empty spaces.

Name	Castor
Place of birth	Nest
Father's name	
Father's job	
Mother's name	Leda
Mother's job	Water nymph
Brother's name	
Sister's name	

The Emperor's lesson

At the beginning of the story we are told that Justinian had twenty cooks who spent their time inventing new and exciting meals for him to eat. Imagine you are one of these cooks. Fill in this blank menu with the most exciting meal that you can invent.

 **MENU**

First course: _____

_____

_____

Main course: _____

_____

Dessert: _____

_____

_____

Draw the food you have chosen on this table.

Patrick and the fox

The fox wants to use the stepping stones to cross the river but he must not step on the wobbly ones.

The fox has been given these clues to help him find the way.

What are the dogs on page 10 called?
What does the fox eat out of?
What are the men on page 11?

Find the words. Show the fox the way to go.

All about foxes

Answer these questions.

1   On page 15 the writer uses two words to name the foxes' homes. They are

_____ and _____ .

2   What is the proper name for a female fox?

_____

3   Why is it safer for foxes to live in the town rather than in the countryside?

_____

_____

4   You are a town fox. You are inviting a country fox to spend the weekend at your den.
        Finish off this invitation.

Dear Fangs,

I do hope you can come and stay this weekend. I will take you out to eat at the

local r_____ d_____ . We can set off whenever we like as there are

no h_____ to chase us. I have recently moved into a very comfortable

g_____ s_____ . It has its own _____

_____ .

I do hope you can come.

Love from

Growler

A kindness rewarded

Write sentences to answer these questions.

1   What was the first meal the young man had in his new home?

_____

_____

2   The fox asked the young man if he could share his food. What else did the fox
     ask the young man?

_____

_____

3   What was the second gift the fox brought to the young man?

_____

_____

4   Why couldn't the evil giantess see the army the fox told her was coming towards
     the castle?

_____

_____

5   Here are some of the gifts that appear in the story.
     Fill in the labels to show who gives them and who receives them.

From:	To:
From:	To:
From:	To:

Danger at sea

Before radios were invented sailors and coastguards used to signal to each other using semaphore flags.

When the flags were held in different positions they spelt out different letters of the alphabet.

H   E   L   P

This person is signalling the word 'Help'.

Here are some more letters in semaphore.

R   N   D   G   T   F   A

Work out what this message says.

☐   ☐   ☐   ☐   ☐   ☐

All about lighthouses

Answer these questions.

1   Why do you think the Romans built towers on which to put their warning fires?

_____

_____

2   Why do lighthouses have to be very strong?

_____

_____

3   What do lighthouse builders do to their lighthouses so that they can be seen during the day?

_____

_____

4   Lighthouses and lightvessels are different.

A lightvessel is found on the_____.

A lighthouse is found on the_____.

5   Imagine that you are in charge of the lighthouses and lightvessels in this area. On the map draw a cross to show where you would build your lighthouse. Draw a circle to show where you would anchor your lightvessel.

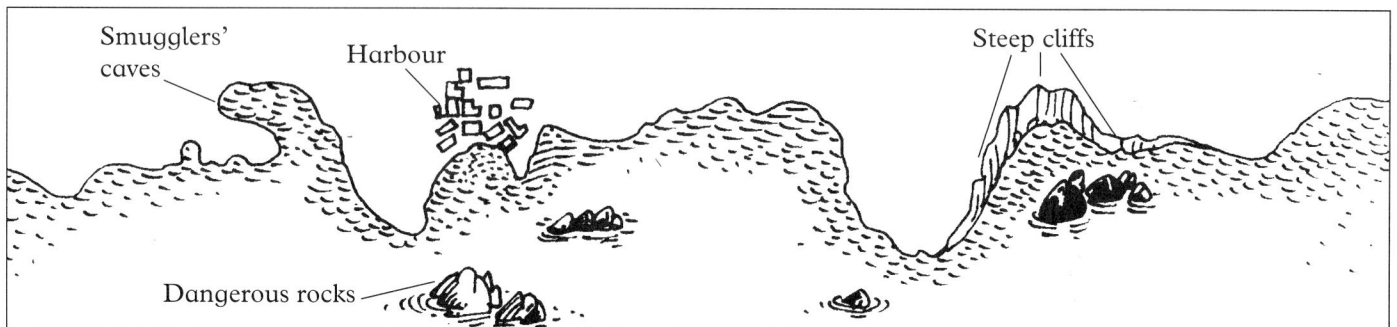

Smugglers' caves   Harbour   Steep cliffs

Dangerous rocks

Grace Darling

Write sentences to answer these questions.

1   What job did Grace Darling's father do?

_____

2   Why couldn't *The Forfarshire* sail away from the dangerous rocks?

_____

_____

3   Why did Mr Darling leave the rowing boat and jump onto the slippery rocks?

_____

_____

4   Why do you think the little rowing boat had to make two trips to the dangerous rocks?

_____

_____

5   Fill in the gaps on the labels.

The rowing boat set out from the _____ Lighthouse.

The Forfarshire had a total of _____ people on board.

_____ people drowned before they could be rescued.

Mr Darling made _____ trips to the rocks.

William and the spell

Draw a circle around the best answer.

1   The television programme William wants to watch is about a

       cat   mouse   wizard   library   rat

2   William is doing a project at school on

       animals   television   wizards   libraries

3   The library allows children this number of books:

       one   two   three   four   five   six

Answer these questions on the story that William reads in his library book.

4   What changes Gary from being a helpful, friendly boy who loves being outdoors, to a rude, lazy boy who stays inside?

       _____

5   What is the first thing that Doctor Magic does to Gary's television?

       _____

6   What is the second thing that Doctor Magic does to Gary's television?

       _____

7   Why did Gary become hungry?

       _____

8   Why does Gary's dad like his son's new shape?

       _____

9   How was Dr Magic's book similar to William's library book?

       _____

William and the spell

Spells often rhyme. This rhyming spell is one that Dr Magic might have used to turn Gary back into a little boy. Finish it off.

Take some pepper, take some flour,
Throw them off a castle tower.
Before they touch the castle moat,
Run downstairs and find a _____.
Before you float far out to sea,
Take a leaf from an apple _____ .
Catch the pepper, drop the flour,
Hold your breath for half an _____.
Before the leaf grows old and brown,
Take it to a foreign _____.
When the townsfolk sneeze and cough
The television will drop _____.

When you have filled in all the missing words use the spaces around the spell to draw pictures of the things you would need to make the spell work.

You could write your own rhyming spell here.

_____

_____

_____

_____

_____

_____

Pages 23–32

Draw a ring around the correct answer.

1	Wizards used magic spells.	True	False
2	The word wizard means wise man.	True	False
3	Wizards solved problems by thinking about them.	True	False
4	Wizards solved problems with their magic wands.	True	False

5   On page 25 the Wizard gives Hans a long list of jobs. The different jobs are divided up by commas.

    'When I get back I shall expect you to have done the washing up, made the beds, chopped the firewood, cooked the dinner and taken the dog for a walk.'

Here are two other lists of jobs. The commas are missing. Copy out each list and put in the missing commas.

'I want the windows cleaned the floor swept the sandwiches cut the cat put outside and the baby fed.'

_____

_____

Hans and Meg tried to help but they did everything wrong. They dusted the dog washed up the toast burnt the plates and took the shelves for a walk.

_____

_____

Space adventure

Answer these questions about the characters.

1   Who was silly when Mrs Patel's class talked about planets?

_____

2   Was it fair when Mrs Patel told Hamid off for talking?   Yes ☐   No ☐

Why do you feel like this?

_____

_____

3   How was Hamid's dad very kind to William and Hamid?

_____

Answer these questions about what happens in the story.

4   What frightened the little green creatures?

_____

5   What did the red beam do?

_____

_____

6   What were the creatures in the spaceship collecting?

_____

7   Why were the creatures interested in Earth?

_____

Space adventure

Here is a picture of the spaceship. The pictures on pages 12 to 18 show some of the rooms inside the spaceship.

Draw a plan of the inside of the spaceship. Make sure you label all the rooms you have read about in the story and put in any others you think would be there.

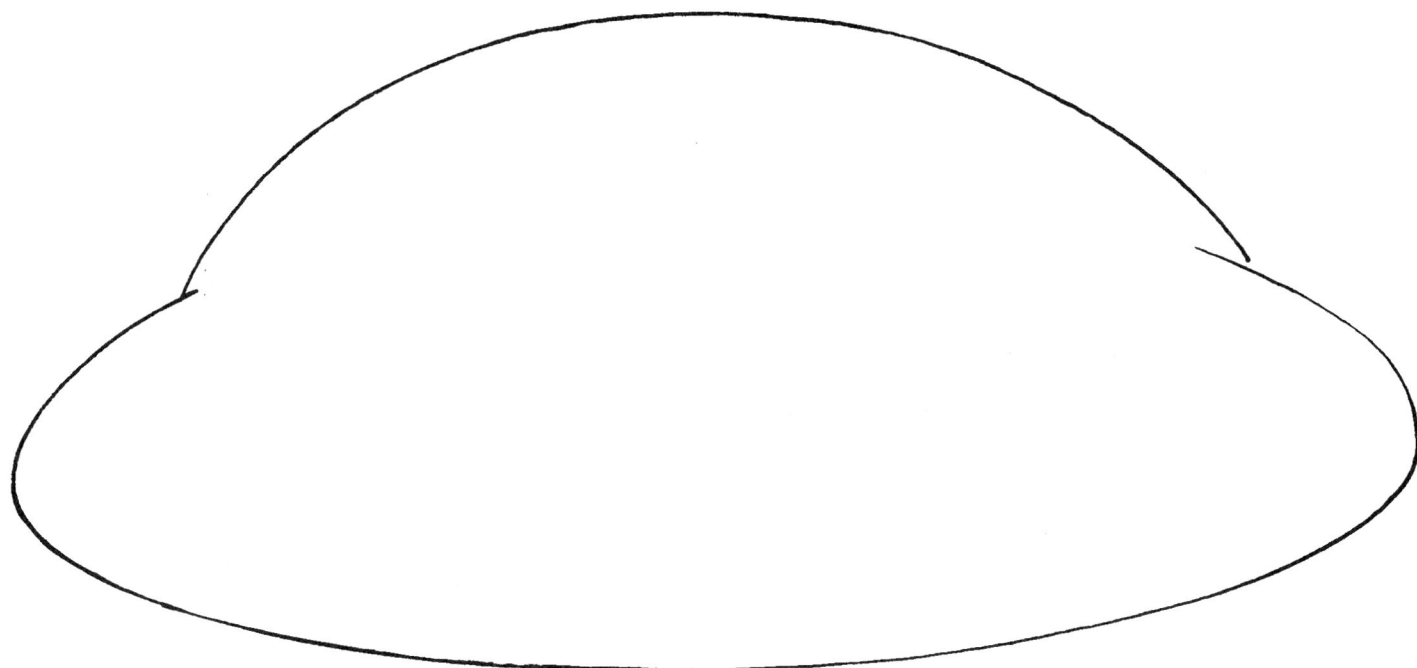

Name of spaceship

Name of spaceship's owners

Now use a coloured pen or pencil to show the route William and Hamid took from the moment they were sucked into the spaceship, carried along the conveyor belt, taken into the control room, put in the answer box, chased along the corridor, fell down the chute and finally escaped from the computer room.

Finally, you can name your spaceship and its owners.

Space

Answer these questions.

1   Birds would be unable to fly in space because there is no

      wind   light   air   sound

2   The only way for humans to go into space is to use

      swans   cannons   aeroplanes   rockets

3   The first man in space was

      Greek   English   Russian   American

4   Which planet is furthest from the Sun?

5   Which planet do you think is hottest?

6   How many miles would you have to travel if you set off from Mars and flew past the Earth to Venus?

7   If you were going to build a place for humans to live on the planet Mars, what special features would you include in your base?

      Draw a picture of your base on a separate sheet.

Karen's adventure

Karen's adventure takes place at her gran's house in the country. Here is a map of the house and garden.

1 Fill in the labels.

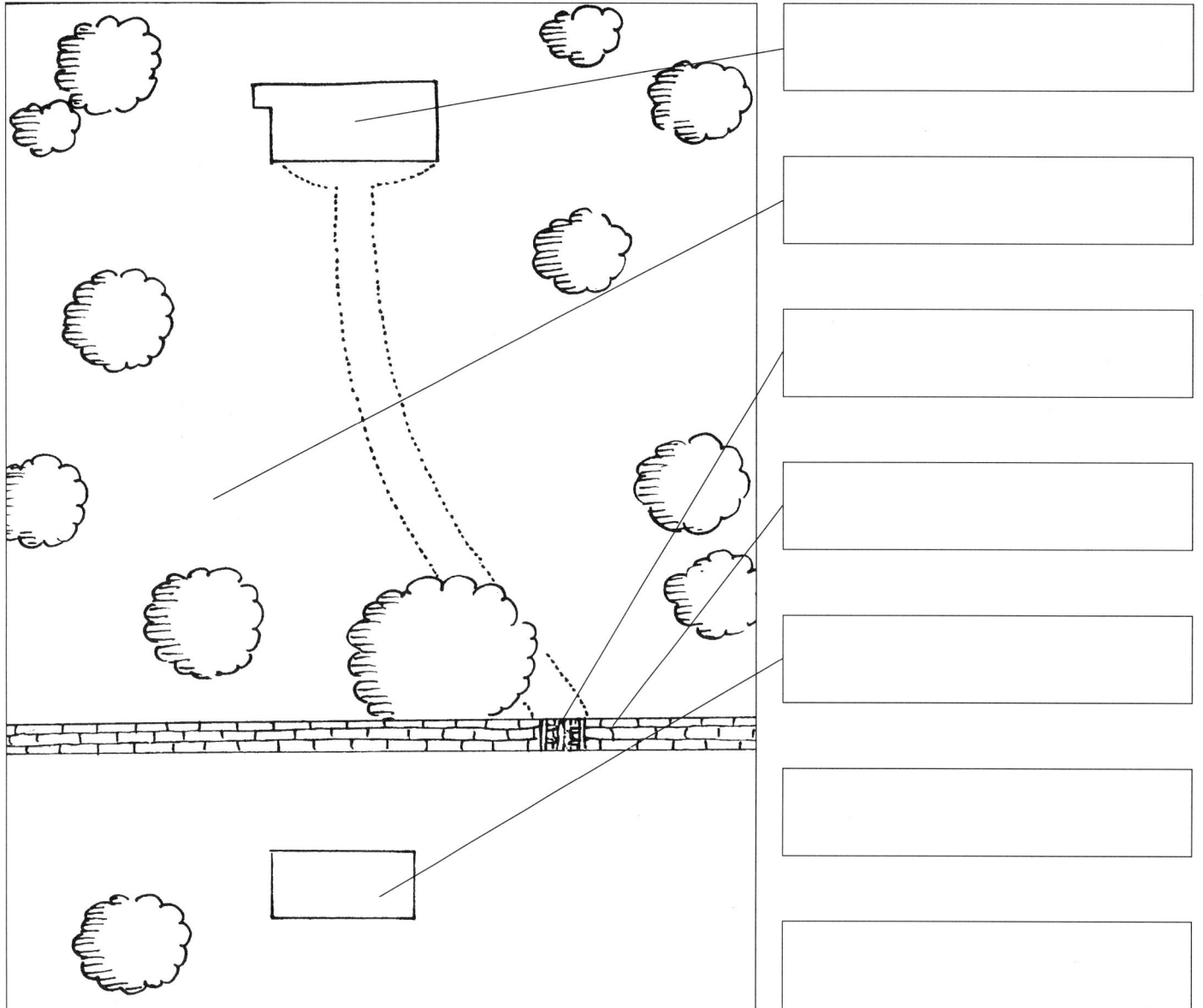

2 Now draw in lines and write labels to show where the tree and ladder were.

All about dragons

Dragons are creatures in legends. That means that there may have been real dragons once but that it is more likely that people made them up.

Imagine your own dragon. Describe it here. Then draw a picture of it.

Hott's first dragon

Answer these questions.

1   Where did Bothva live?

       Denmark   England   Norway   France   Scotland

2   On page 26 the writer uses a special word that means the handle of a sword. That word is _____.

3   What did the King do that showed he was very pleased to see Bothva in his Hall?

_____

4   Why couldn't Hott run away when Bothva said he was taking him with him to kill the dragon?

_____

5   Here is a song which was sung in Hott's honour. Some of the rhyming words have vanished. Fill in the gaps using words that rhyme with the last word in the line above.

Hott was brave, Hott was strong,
Hott killed the dragon that had done us _____.
Hott took his chance, Hott took his sword,
Hott wasn't scared when the dragon _____.

6   You could finish off this poem about a dragon.

Be careful of a dragon, he'll breathe out fire.
If he says he doesn't, he's probably a liar.
Be careful of a dragon _____

_____

Kate's garden

Here are four different shapes.

A square

A cylinder

A triangle

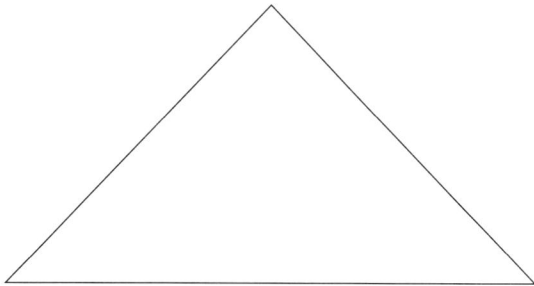

A rectangle

Write inside the correct shape:

1   Something on page 2 that you would find in a cylinder.
2   Something on page 2 that Mum used to make two squares.
3   Something on page 5 that has a roof like a triangle.
4   Something on page 7 that has the shape of a rectangle.

All about seeds

Answer the questions.

1   What are the two things that every seed contains?

2   Why do seeds have tough outside skins?

_____

3   How does moisture reach the seed?

_____

4   Fill in the gaps in this sum:

| seed | + | a | + | w | + | moisture | = growth |

5   Circle the correct word that means begin to grow.

germs   germinate   geranium   gem

6   In which season of the year do most seeds start their growth?

winter   spring   summer   autumn

7   The seeds of some plants have special names. Use a dictionary to help you join the

right seed to the right plant.

apple	grain
oak	conker
plum	nut
wheat	pip
horse chestnut	acorn
hazel	stone

The gift of corn

Answer these questions.

1 Why couldn't the Chief and his tribe catch any fish?

_____

_____

2 Why did the Chief stay behind?

_____

3 What happened to Red Feather after the wrestling match?

_____

4 Red Feather is like the corn. He is small but strong, he has golden skin and he wears a red feather that looks like the red plume on the top of the corn.

Think of another plant, a carrot perhaps, or an apple tree. Draw a picture of that plant then, next to it, draw a picture of a person who looks like that plant.

Monkey business

Answer these questions by reading pages 1 to 11.

1   Look at the picture of Mr Jolly's house on page 1. Mr Jolly is very interested in

_____.

2   If you read the words on page 2 you will discover that Mr Jolly is very interested in

_____.

3   How does Mr Jolly begin his day's work at the zoo?

_____

4   Why do you think Mr Jolly leaves Chuckles to the end?

_____

_____

5   Tick the sentence you think is correct.

Chuckles laughs because he thinks Mr Jolly's jokes are funny.
Chuckles laughs because Mr Jolly is laughing.
Chuckles laughs because he hasn't heard the jokes before.

6   Mr Jolly likes Chuckles, but he makes Chuckles sad. How does Mr Jolly make Chuckles sad?

_____

_____

7   On page 7 there is a question. It has a question mark at the end, like this ?. Find the question, then make up some questions of your own, using question marks.

_____

_____

_____

A chimp for a day

Answer these questions.

1   What was Simon's favourite animal?

_____

2   Why do you think Simon stopped talking English?

_____

3   Simon had to do something in the car that a chimp wouldn't do. What was it?

_____

4   What do you think Simon should have done if he had wanted Mrs Perry to buy him
     an ice-cream?

_____

_____

5   What makes Simon start speaking in English?

_____

_____

6   What happens after the story ends?

     Fill in what you think Simon, Simon's mum and Simon's dad said next. Don't forget
     to put in the speech marks.

     _____, laughed Simon's mum.

     _____, said Simon.

     Simon's dad stuck a sausage on his fork and passed it to Simon and said,

     _____

     _____.

Pages 18–27

Answer these questions.

1   Tick the two boxes that you think explain best why people think chimpanzees behave like humans.

      ☐   They show their feelings in their faces.

      ☐   They climb trees.

      ☐   They eat mainly nuts, berries, fruit and leaves.

      ☐   They can use simple tools.

      ☐   They make loud barking noises.

2   Why do chimpanzees climb trees?

_____

3   The Howler Monkey was given its name because of the noise it makes. Why do you think the Spider Monkey was given its name?

_____

_____

4   In 'The monkey and the shark' sometimes the characters are clever, at other times they are foolish.

The monkey was foolish when it _____.

The shark was foolish when it _____.

The monkey was clever when it _____.

The shark was clever when it _____.

The playroom

Draw a circle around the word that you think gives the best answer.

1   Jo's great-grandfather lived in

      England   Scotland   Ireland   Wales

2   In the game Jo's great-grandfather played as a boy he pretended he was imprisoned in the

      clock   doll's house   tower   tent   train

3   In the game Jo's great-grandfather played as a boy he was kept prisoner by

      Jo   Sir Edmund   the Red Baron   the white knights

Answer these questions on what happens in the story.

4   How does Jo change when she enters the playroom at night?

_____

5   Who else has been affected in this way?

_____

6   How does Jo disguise Sir Edmund?

_____

7   What spoilt Jo's disguise for Sir Edmund?

_____

8   Why does it take some time for the Red Baron to enter the room at the top of the tower?

_____

9   What is the bravest thing the Red Baron does?

_____

The playroom

Answer these questions about the way the artist and the writer have created the story.

1   Look carefully at the pictures on pages 2 to 6. What has the artist made the toy castle look like?

_____

2   What makes the train work?

_____

3   On page 20 the writer uses two exclamation marks.
     'Bombs away!' laughed Great-grandfather.
     'Never!' said the Baron.

     The writer has used exclamation marks because he wants to show that these characters in the story are speaking in an excited, loud or angry manner.

     Find three more sentences in the book which end with exclamation marks.
     Write them here.

_____

_____

_____

_____

_____

_____

_____

Castles

Answer these questions.

1   Here is a map of a castle. Put the words below the map into the correct boxes.

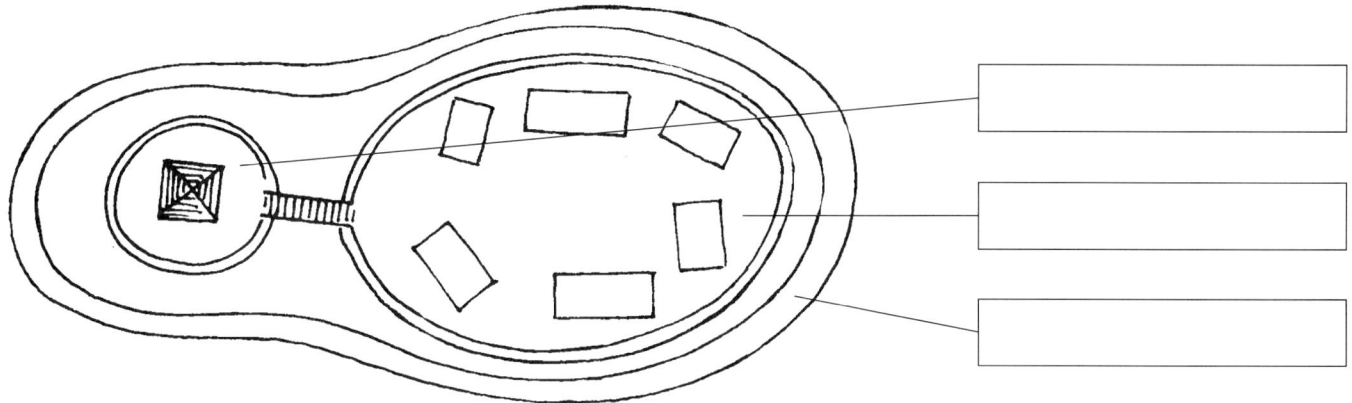

bailey   motte   moat

2   If an enemy army camps outside a castle and stops food and water going in and the people inside coming out, a _____ is taking place.

3   Castles became useless when _____ was invented.

4   Here are two lists: one gives the names of different people who lived in Britain, the other gives the names of the types of defences they built. Draw a line to connect the right people to the right defences.

Romans	hill forts
Celts	motte and bailey
Normans	army camps

5   A word on page 24 that means defend is _____.

A word on page 26 that means hill is _____.

A word on page 27 that means captured is _____.

In the snow

Part of the story has been turned into a poem.
It has five verses and each verse has two lines.

The last word on the second line of each verse is missing. It has to rhyme with the last word in the first line. You will find the rhyming words on the pages.

Off to the park the children go,

They want to play in the crisp, white _____

page 1

Hamid starts them off with a mighty shove,

The snow creeps into William's _____

page 2

They race down the hill to the water's edge,

William's fingers grip the _____

page 3

They jump in the air, flying, gliding,

They crash back down, slipping, _____

page 9

They are covered in snow, Hamid laughs,

William's glad he wore his _____

page 2

All about snow and ice

Answer these questions.

1   Tick those that contain water.

      rivers   lakes   air   steam   ice

2   What gas does water turn into when it's heated by the sun?

      _____

3   What does water vapour turn into when it is frozen?

      _____

4   Although no ice crystals are ever the same shape they do have one thing in common. What is it?

      _____

5   Imagine it has snowed in a country where snow has never been seen before. Choose one of the following activities and write a set of simple instructions on how to do it, to send to the children there.

      ■ Building a snowman   ■ Going sledging
      ■ Having a snowball fight   ■ Going ice skating

Instructions for _____

Step 1 _____

Step 2 _____

Step 3 _____

Step 4 _____

Pages 20–32

Answer these questions on 'Why the bear sleeps through the winter'.

1   Why had the bridge been washed away?

_____

_____

2   Why wouldn't the horse take the man across the river?

_____

_____

3   Why does the bear think it won't be easy for him to carry the man across the river?

_____

_____

4   How did Ukku reward the bear?

_____

_____

This question is about 'How the chipmunk got its stripes'.

What might have made:

■ the zebra's stripes?

■ the leopard's spots?

■ the robin's red breast?

Write the story to go with one of the pictures on a separate sheet.

The catch

Use each of these letters once to answer the questions.

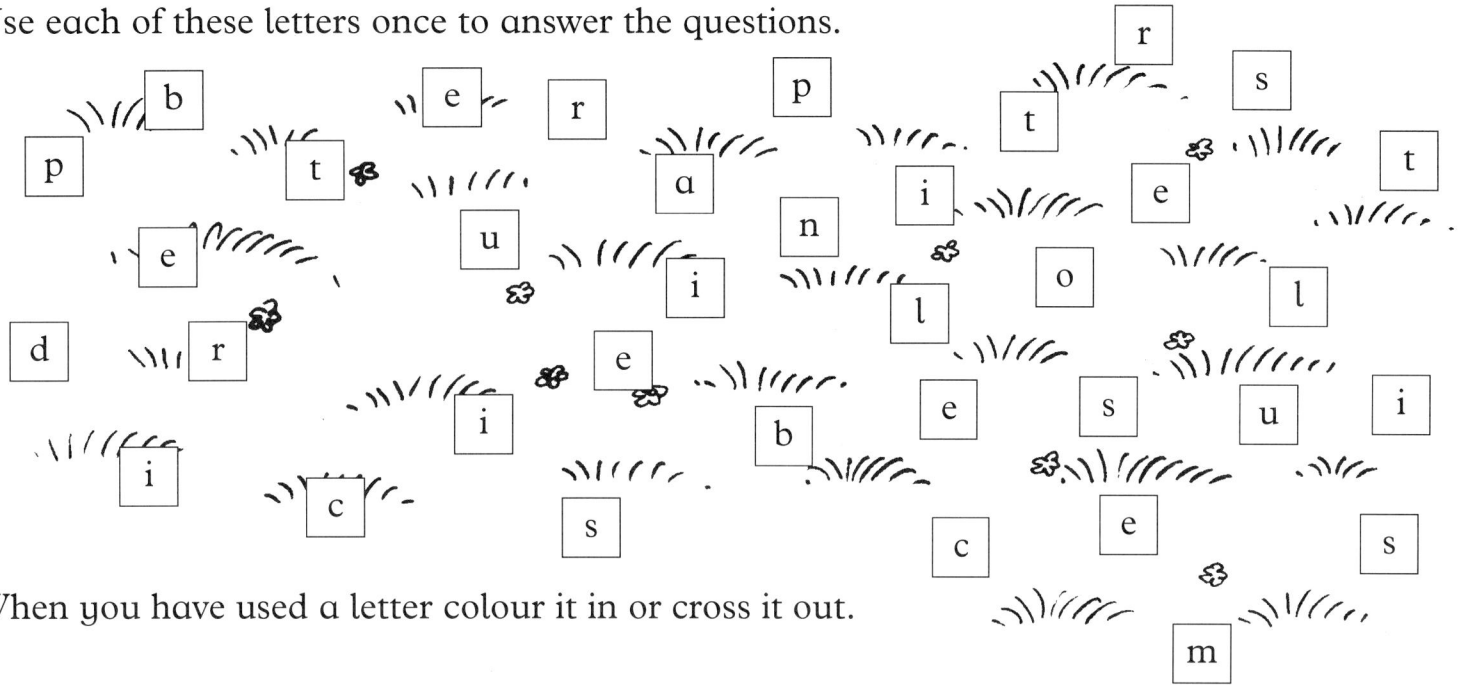

b p t e r p r s t a n i e t u e i o l d r l e e s u i i b s c c e s m

When you have used a letter colour it in or cross it out.

1   What is the word on page 1 that means answered?

☐ ☐ ☐ ☐ ☐ ☐ ☐ ☐

2   What is the word on page 6 that means sad?

☐ ☐ ☐ ☐ ☐ ☐ ☐ ☐ ☐ ☐

3   What is the word on page 10 that means an outdoor meal?

☐ ☐ ☐ ☐ ☐ ☐

4   What is the word on page 13 that means replacement?

☐ ☐ ☐ ☐ ☐ ☐ ☐ ☐ ☐ ☐ ☐

5   What is the word on page 17 that means went up?

☐ ☐ ☐ ☐

Chinese horoscopes

Answer these questions.

1   Which month of which year were you born?

Month: _____   Year: _____

Look at the chart at the bottom of page 25.

What is your Chinese horoscope sign? _____

2   Alastair never misses a day at school because he never seems to be ill. He doesn't say much but sometimes he stays in at lunch-time to finish the work he began in the morning. Which animal do you think ruled the year he was born in?

_____

3   A new ruler has come to a country that is always being attacked by enemies and has great difficulties in feeding its people. What animal do you think the people of that country hope was ruling when their new ruler was born?

_____

4   Anna was born in the year of the rabbit.
     Ben was born in the year of the dragon.
     Karen was born in the year of the horse.
     David was born in the year of the dog.

     Who would you choose:

     ■ to look after a new pupil? _____

     ■ to water the plants? _____

     ■ to lead the running team? _____

     ■ to tidy the classroom? _____

5   Under which animal sign would you like to have been born? _____

     Why did you choose this sign? _____

     _____

The race

1   Why were the animals making such a terrible noise?

_____

2   Which of the animals do you think was the cleverest?

_____

3   What did this animal do to make you choose it as the cleverest?

_____

_____

4   Draw a map in the box. Show the mountain, the forest, the rice fields, the great river
      and the winning post. Draw a dotted line that shows the route the animals took.
      Around the edge draw the twelve animals that took part in the race.

The Great Race

William and the ghost

To fill in the crossword on the front of this treasure chest use the clues below.

Across

1   Read page 3. What sort of rooms does the castle have?

5   Read page 7. The children in the class have to draw the most _____ thing they see.

7   Read page 5. What is the name for a person who lives in a monastery?

10 Read page 8. What does William choose to draw?

11 Read page 13. What are the plates in the chest made from?

12 Put in the missing word from page 15: Let __ see.

Down

1   Read page 1. What doesn't William want to miss?

2   Read page 3. What vanished with Earl Gloomy?

3   Read page 13. There were lots of these in the treasure chest.

4   Read page 6. What fuel was used on the castle fires?

6   Read page 11. What was at the bottom of the steps?

8   Read page 10. What came out of the small door?

9   Read page 10. What part of the armour moved?

All about ghosts

Here is a plan of the centre of a town. Next to the plan are the four ghosts that haunt certain buildings in the town. Draw a line from each ghost to the building where you think it would be found.

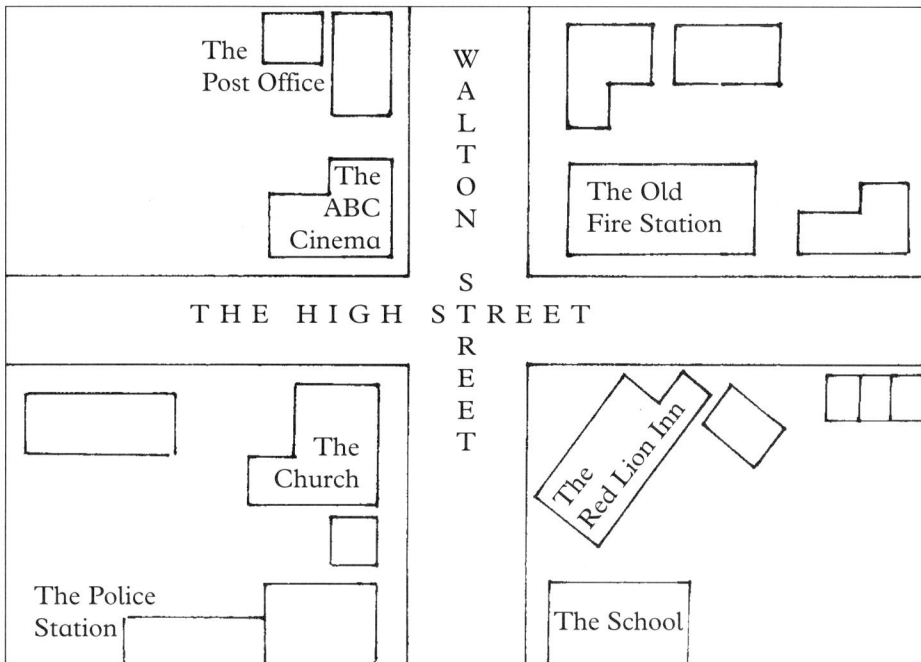

Choose one of the buildings which hasn't been named. Decide what sort of building it is and label it. Then decide what sort of ghost haunts this building and draw a picture of it below.

Miss Terry's holiday

Answer the questions.

1   Number these events in the order that they happened.
     The first one has been done for you.

☐   Miss Terry knocked on the cottage door.

☐   Miss Terry had a picnic.

1   Miss Terry set off for Devon.

☐   Miss Terry's car wouldn't start.

☐   Miss Terry went into the ruined cottage.

☐   It began to rain.

☐   The little girl offered Miss Terry some cake.

2   What was Miss Terry doing when she first saw the cottage?

_____

3   Why did Miss Terry wake up?

_____

4   What did Miss Terry hope to find in the cottage?

_____

5   What do you think happens to the little girl when Miss Terry says goodbye to her?
     Start your story when Miss Terry walks off down the lane.

_____

_____

_____

_____

William and the mouse

Eenor the mouse has to escape from the cat! He runs into a room full of letters. There are seven doors to choose from. Only one door leads to safety.

Read the clues. Draw a ring round the words. The right answers will lead Eenor to the right door.

Clues

Page 1:   William's mum won't be back for _____ .

Page 2:   The biggest piece of furniture in the room is the _____ .

Page 3:   Once the boys had searched the room they started all over _____ .

Page 4:   When mice eat they take a little _____ .

Page 5:   Turn around the place where Eenor lives.

Page 6:   What noise does the garden gate make?

```
          1                    2
    a  g  e  s  a  d  c  a  t  r  y
    b  i  e  o  o  t  h  e  s  a  t
    c  a  l  f  z  f  a  n  e  s  t
    t  b  l  a  g  a  i  n  z  c  o   3
    c  a  g  e  a  f  r  i  p  a  v
    s  d  o  q  l  r  u  b  o  a  t
    i  r  a  u  d  a  e  b  e  a  t
    m  o  t  i  p  i  c  l  o  c  k
    p  d  a  t  c  a  g  e  h  e  n
 7  h  o  m  e  l  h  e  l  e  n  a
    x  c  h  a  i  r  g  c  t  h  e
    o  k  z  a  c  a  c  l  i  c  k   4
    e  y  e  d  k  z  l  a  n  e  p
          6           5
```

Which door will lead Eenor to safety? [   ]

All about mice

Answer these questions.

1   Where did the first mice live?

        Europe   England   China   Egypt

2   What is another name for the Woodmouse?

        _____

3   Why do you think many mice like to live near humans?

        _____

4   What do mice use paper, straw and wool for?

        _____

5   Find a word on page 8 that means shy. _____

6   Explain how a mouse could destroy a house.

        _____

        _____

7   Look in other books and find out two interesting facts about harvest mice.
        Write them here.

        _____

        _____

        _____

        _____

Yin Ling's tale

1 Why did the boy throw the ball at the breakfast table?

_____

2 How can you tell that Yin Ling has shrunk down to the size of a mouse?

_____

_____

3 Why do you think the cat wanted to knock the tins of cat food off the shelf?

_____

_____

4 Imagine you fall asleep at school and wake up to find you have turned into a mouse. Here is a page from the diary you kept when you were that mouse. Fill in the details about the rest of your day.

Monday

morning

My teacher was very surprised when she called me up to read to her.

The rest of the class _____

_____

afternoon

_____

_____

evening

_____

_____

The snow storm

Draw a circle around the word that gives the best answer.

1   At the start of the story Rob and Becky's mum was at the

        farm   cottage   hospital   station

2   At the end of the story Rob and Becky's mum was at the

        farm   cottage   hospital   station

3   The only character in the story who is not a member of the same family is

    Mum   Dad   baby   Tessa   Becky   Rob

4   The telephone wires were broken by the

    snow   wind   tree   children   tractor

Answer these questions about the characters.

5   Who do you think is the bravest person in the story?

    Tessa   Dad   Rob   Becky   Mum

6   Why did you choose this person?

_____

_____

7   Give two reasons why Rob was so tired on page 17.

_____

_____

8   Why did the children stop playing snowballs?

_____

_____

The snow storm

1   Number these events in the right order. The first one has been done for you.

☐ The children play snowballs.

1 Tessa arrives.

☐ The children try to reach the farm.

☐ Tessa makes cocoa.

☐ The children eat their meal.

☐ The children are rescued.

☐ Dad leaves the cottage.

2   Write a Christmas poem to fit inside this Christmas tree.

Pages 25–32

Draw a circle round the correct answers to these questions on 'Stars'.

1   The sun is a

meteor   comet   star   planet

2   The sun looks bigger to us than other stars because it is the

biggest   smallest   nearest   fastest

3   Another name for a shooting star is

meteor   comet   star   planet

4   Draw a line from each of these words to show if they belong to the meteor or to the comet.

gas   dust   rock   lucky   metal   unlucky

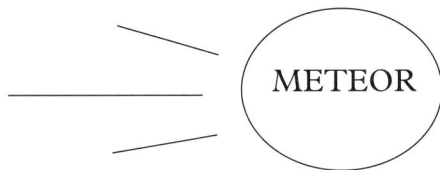

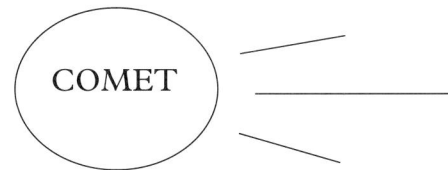

METEOR   COMET

Answer these questions on 'The star child'.

5   What was the one thing that proved to the old people that the boy in the woodcutter's house was their son?

_____

6   What was the only thing that could make the star child and his parents happy?

_____

7   Why do you think the boy's parents had searched for him dressed like beggars?

_____

The secret cave

Draw a circle around the word that gives the best answer.

1   The smugglers liked the village because of the

   pub   caves   coastguards   sand

2   The favourite pets of the smugglers were

   worms   mice   cats   parrots

3   The chief smuggler was called

   Blackbeard   Irons   Hood   Hamid

4   Hamid and William escaped from the ship with the help of

   coastguards   smugglers   mice   Mrs Hood   pirates

Answer these questions about the way the story is written.

5   The story starts with a story-teller. Who is he?

_____

6   If you were the chief smuggler would you have allowed William and Hamid a candle?

   Yes ☐   No ☐

   Why did you choose that answer?

_____

_____

7   Why did the two smugglers in the bigger rowing boat sink?

_____

8   Why do you think Blackbeard told the coastguards that William and Hamid were smugglers?

_____

_____

The secret cave

1   William and Hamid escaped because the mice liked cheese. What do you think might have happened if the mice didn't like cheese and didn't eat through the ropes? Would William and Hamid have escaped? Do you think they might have joined the crew of the smuggling ship? Carry on this version of the story.

'All we can do now is wait,' said Hamid.
They waited and waited, but the mice didn't seem to like the smell of cheese. The ropes remained tight around their wrists.

_____

_____

_____

You can continue the story on another sheet if you need to.

2   'The secret cave' has been made into a film. You have been asked to design a poster to advertise it. Fill in the gaps and draw a picture that shows what you think is the best part of the story. Remember that your poster must make people want to see the film!

The Secret Cave!

The exciting story of _____

and their fight against _____ !

Shiver when you see the dreadful _____ !

Cheer when the _____ !

At a cinema near you

The phantom ship

Answer the questions.

1   Why did Ben wish he had stayed at home?

_____

_____

2   Why was Ben surprised when he went into the Captain's cabin with the soup?

_____

_____

3   Why do you think the Dutchman saved the cook's life?

_____

_____

4   What were the two things that appeared on the pirates' flag?

_____ and _____

5   Why do you think the guns on The Sea Lion didn't do any harm to the ship that attacked the pirates?

_____

_____

6   The story doesn't say why the Dutchman had to sail the seas for ever. Why do you think the Dutchman and his phantom ship had been punished in this way?

_____

_____

_____

The island

Answer these questions.

1   Why have Liz and her dad come to Scotland?

_____

2   List three things Liz and her dad always do on the second day of their stay at the
     cottage by the loch.

     ■   _____

     ■   _____

     ■   _____

3   Why does Mrs McKay like living on the island?

     _____

     _____

4   Why did Mr Campbell want to build a theme park on the island where Mrs McKay
     lived?

     _____

     _____

5   Why didn't Mrs McKay want a theme park on the island?

     _____

     _____

6   What plans does Mr Campbell have for the ruined castle on the island?

     _____

     _____

The island

On pages 9 to 11 Mrs McKay tells Liz the story about the monster in the loch.

Draw a picture that shows what the wicked laird looked like after he had turned into the monster. Make sure you use the information in the story to help you.

This map shows the area where Mrs McKay lives. Draw lines from the words on the right to the places on the map.

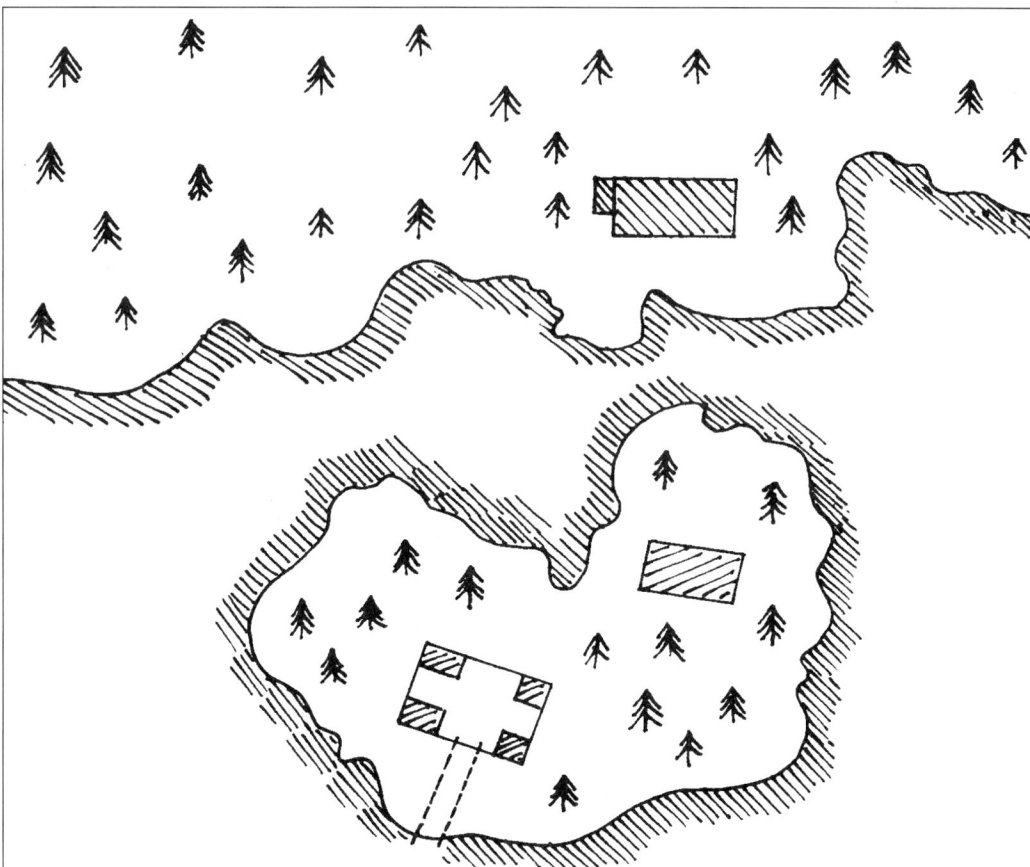

| castle |
| tunnel |
| pottery |
| cottage |
| loch |
| mainland |
| cove |

Pages 22–32

Answer these questions about pages 22 to 25.

1	The Giant Squid is a real creature.	True	False
2	The Loch Ness Monster has been captured.	True	False
3	Mermaids might have been seals.	True	False

4   What do you think the island in the story 'A strange island' might have been?

_____

Answer these questions on 'The water horse'.

5   Farmers wanted the water horse's land because it was

fertile   wet   beautiful   expensive

6   When the water horse changed from being a young man and chased the farmer's daughter, he turned himself into a

lion   eagle   tiger   bull   horse   bear

7   What were the two sounds that Janet heard that warned her the water horse was getting closer and closer?

_____   _____

8   What could have happened to give the story a happy ending? Write your ideas here.

_____

_____

_____

The chimney sweep

Draw a circle around the best answer.

1   Mr Webster treated Jake   kindly   badly   sensibly   fairly

2   Slim was Jake's   friend   helper   dog   enemy

3   Webster didn't let Jake in the cart because the brushes were

        heavy   long   old   dirty   broken

4   Webster spoke pleasantly to the housemaid because he was

        hungry   kind   greedy   tired   polite

5   The word urchin is used on page 1. An urchin is a

        poor boy   friendly dog   cruel man   rich boy

6   When Jake sees daylight through the chimney pot on page 10 he decides to

        escape   find a place to rest   get a better view   jump

7   On page 6 Mr Webster gasped. On page 15 Jake gasped.

When they gasped they were both

        angry   frightened   amazed   worried   shocked

8   Jake almost fell off the roof because

        he was afraid of heights   he slipped   he fell asleep

        Slim shouted at him   Mr Webster shouted at him

9   Jake had dreamt about being a chimney sweep because

        it was his job   he had seen a painting

        he had seen a television programme   he had found a secret passage

Living in the past

Answer these questions.

1   Number these instructions in the correct order for a servant about to make a fire.

☐   Light the fire.

☐   Clear away the ashes.

☐   Put the dry wood and coal on the fire.

☐   Fill the coal bucket.

2   If you had to work in Victorian times which of these jobs would you choose to do?

chimney sweep   coal miner   horse minder

Imagine you are living in Victorian times and that you are doing the job you chose. Fill in this postcard so that you can warn your class about the things they will have to do if they follow you.

FROM:

JOB:

This is terrible! I have to _____

_____

_____

_____

_____

TO: _____

CLASS: _____

SCHOOL: _____

_____

_____

The little match girl

Here is the start of the story:

> It was New Year's Eve. All over the city people were hurrying home to their warm houses. Everybody wanted to celebrate the end of the old year and the beginning of the new. 'Happy New Year!' they called to one another. Everywhere there was laughter.

You will see these kinds of punctuation in the passage:

- capital letters
- full stops
- speech marks
- an exclamation mark

Here are two other passages. Copy them out, putting in all the missing punctuation. You will need a question mark too.

please will you buy my matches whispered the little girl she could hardly get the words out because she was shivering so much

the little girl struck a third match in its glow she saw the gentle smiling face of her grandmother, the only person who had ever loved her and been kind to her grandmother gasped the little girl i thought you had left me forever please stay with me

_____

_____

_____

_____

_____

_____

_____

Further activities

Many different themes and topics are covered by the stories in *Oxford Reading Tree*. This section contains ideas for developing three of these topics so as to provide a framework for a variety of cross-curricular activities.

Tricks and disguises

The following *Oxford Reading Tree* books could be read as part of this topic:

The catch (Jackdaws); *The school play, The jokers,* and *The playroom (More Jackdaws)*

Discussion

Tricks: Talk about tricks the children have played on others, tricks that have been played on them, and tricks they would like to play. Do they enjoy being tricked? Do the people they play tricks on enjoy being tricked? Have they seen people being tricked on television? Did they think it was fair? When do tricks become unfair? Can some tricks be cruel?

Disguises: Ask the children why they think people might need to disguise themselves. Why do clowns disguise themselves? Why do famous people disguise themselves? How would the children disguise themselves? What would they use in their disguise?

Fancy dress: Ask the children if they have seen a carnival procession or if they have ever worn fancy dress, or a costume, in a parade, a play or to a party. What would they like to dress up as?

Writing

Rudyard Kipling's *Just So Stories* include stories about how some animals acquired their distinctive features, for example, how the leopard got its spots or the rhinoceros its skin. These features are often forms of camouflage or disguise (see the Science activity below). These tales make good starting points for children's writing. They might like to write stories to explain How the snails got their shells, or How the kangaroo got her pouch.

Art

You could ask the children either to bring in photographs of themselves, or else to draw pictures of themselves. They could use coloured pictures made from their own drawings or cut from magazines and pieces of cloth, coloured paper, wool, string, beads, silver foil, etc. to make fancy dress collages around the pictures of their faces. When they are all completed display as a class carnival.

Design Technology

One of the oldest and most famous stories involving a trick is the tale of the Wooden or Trojan Horse. Designing, making and painting a model of the Wooden Horse is a good starting point for a Design Technology project.

The main body can be made from thin card, such as cereal packets. The cardboard tubes from lavatory or kitchen rolls make sturdy legs and necks. Discuss whether the children wish to make their horses move. Wheels can be made from cotton reels faced with cardboard, or plastic bottle tops glued together. Another method would be to use pencils as rollers: make a line of pencils, then as the horse is pushed along take the pencils from the back and add them to the line at the front. Some children may want to make a little door in the body of the horse so that it can be opened, revealing the Greeks hiding inside.

Maths

Pictures and models of the Wooden Horse provide an interesting starting point for investigations of shape and space. The body and the legs of the horse, for example, might well be cylinders, the legs might rest on a rectangular box. Making a cylinder is a particularly interesting exercise as it starts with a two-dimensional shape – a rectangle – which is then manipulated to form a three-dimensional shape – a cylinder. This transformation is a useful opportunity for introducing vocabulary such as sides/edges and surfaces.

Science

Many living creatures disguise themselves. Some species of butterfly, such as The Peacock, have patterns on their wings that resemble eyes. When these butterflies are alarmed they spread their wings so that the sudden appearance of the 'eyes' will frighten their enemies.

You could build up a picture display of animals, plants and birds which use colour, form or sound to pretend to be something else. Some of these may use camouflage as a way to stay concealed from enemies. One good example of a plant disguise is the bee orchid which uses its flowers to mimic the insects it wants to attract. Many birds are good mimics. The children may have encountered mynah birds, macaws and budgies which can mimic the human voice. Show the children that it is possible for humans to mimic birds' calls as well – try rattling a matchbox to attract magpies!

Music

Composers sometimes mimic the sounds of animals or birds in their compositions. Play the children a recording of Saint-Saen's 'Carnival of the Animals'. Let them try to guess the creatures he is depicting in each section.

Drama/Science

Ask the children if they have ever watched a conjuror, magician or an illusionist perform. Do they know any tricks themselves? Do they know the secrets behind any tricks?

Mastering a simple illusion, and then rehearsing how to present the trick effectively in front of an audience, is a good way for children to learn the importance of thorough preparation before performance. The ability to perform a successful trick is also a remarkable confidence builder.

This simple, but effective, trick may also be used as part of a scientific investigation!

◆ Pour water into a jam jar until it is about two thirds full.
◆ Place an ice cube (as cold as possible) in the water.
◆ Tell the audience that you will lift the ice cube out of the jam jar using only a straight piece of string. You won't touch the ice cube and you won't loop the string.
◆ Dip the string in the water. Place the wet end of the string on the floating ice cube.
◆ Tell the audience the ice cube will only rise out of the jam jar if they all concentrate on the ice for ten seconds. They must shut their eyes and count to ten.
◆ As the audience do this pour salt onto the spot where the string is resting on the ice cube. The salt will make the string and the ice stick together.
◆ When the audience open their eyes you should be able to lift the string and the ice cube out of the water.

This trick works because the salt raises the temperature on the surface of the ice cube, causing it to melt. Once the salt is dissolved, however, the cold water surrounding the ice cube and the ice cube itself, re-freeze the thin film of water which has formed around the string, thus fixing it with ice to the cube.

Book list

Story books

Allan Ahlberg *Mr Creep the Crook, Mrs Jolly's Joke Shop* (Viking)
R and D Armitage *The birthday spell* (Hippo books)
Vivian French and Chris Fisher *Hedgehogs and the Big Bag* (Puffin)
Mary Hooper *Two Naughty Angels Down to Earth* (Bloomsbury)
Alexander McCall Smith *The Princess Trick* (Blackie)
Geraldine McCaughrean *The Odyssey* (Oxford University Press)
John Ryan *Captain Pugwash and the Fancy Dress Party* (Puffin)
David Thomson *Danny Fox, Danny Fox Meets a Stranger* (Puffin)
Alison Uttley *Little red fox* (Young Puffin)
Brian Wildsmith *The hare and the tortoise* (Oxford University Press)
Anansi, Turtle and Pigeon (Share a story series, Ginn)
The magic pot (Share a story series, Ginn)
SOS for Rita, Happy Christmas, Rita! (Hamish Hamilton)
Tricks and disguises also feature in such fairy stories as:
Little Riding Hood, Puss in Boots, Snow White, Jack and the Beanstalk and *The Seven Little Kids.*

Poetry books

From the *Oxford Reading Tree*
Wizard Poems (*More Jackdaws* poetry)

Information books

Wendy Baker *The Dressing up Book* (Franklin Watts)
Gill Dickinson *Fancy Dress* (Apple Press)
Jon Mayled *Carnival* (Wayland)
Chris Oxlade *Science Magic with: Air, Light, Forces, Water, Magnets* (Franklin Watts)

Buildings

The following *Oxford Reading Tree* books could be read as part of this topic:

Karen's adventure and *William and the ghost* (*Jackdaws*); *The playroom, The island* and *The chimney sweep* (*More Jackdaws*)
(See also *Fact Finders*, Unit C: *Houses and homes*, More Unit C: *Build a model of your school.*)

Discussion

Choose a building: You could encourage the children to talk about buildings they know well. As a class choose one particular building which everyone will be able to look at in some detail. Your own school would be fine.

Purpose: What is the chosen building used for? What about other buildings in the area? What are they used for?

Location: Why is the chosen building in this particular place? Are there any other similar buildings nearby?

Writing

Ask the children to imagine they are a house as it is being built. What do they think it feels like to grow out of the ground? Can they only see when the windows are put in place? Do they only come really alive when the electricity is passing through their wires and the water is being pumped through their pipes? Write the house's autobiography.

Science

Having agreed on a particular building to study the children could investigate how it was built. What materials can the children identify? Can they find bricks, concrete, glass, steel, tiles and wood? Can the children find any evidence of construction techniques, for example, metal girders bolted together, glass held in by putty or slotted into metal frames, sections of brickwork, pieces of wood that are jointed together?

You could help your class make a senses census. To do this they could use a simple worksheet:

Material:	brick
Touch:	rough
Taste:	DO NOT DO!
Sight:	red/rectangle/bumpy
Hearing:	dull sound when tapped
Smell:	none

Maths

While looking round the chosen building the children will be able to identify many different geometric shapes, such as triangular roofs, square windows and cylindrical columns. If the children look at pictures of other types of building they will be able to see many other shapes: there are sides, edges and triangles in the Pyramids; there may be cubes, cuboids, rectangles, even hexagons or pentagons in a large house.

Gather a large pile of pictures of buildings cut from magazines. Ask the class to identify particular shapes that have been used in the buildings. The children could cut these shapes out, stick them onto card or stiff paper and then mix them up to make fantasy buildings for a class display.

History

When was the chosen building constructed? Help the children to look for clues. Is there a date anywhere on the building? Are there any clues to be found in the materials that were used? Ask the children to ask their families if any of them know anything about the building. Perhaps some of them helped to build it. Perhaps they used, or still use, it. Are there members of the children's families who could tell any interesting stories about the building?

The pictures in some of the *Jackdaws* stories, for example, 'William and the ghost' and 'Miss Terry's story', contain many details of historical interiors, including suits of armour, candles, carved furniture, oil lamps, and a kitchen range. You could use examples like these to make a picture museum.

Head a sheet of paper with a picture of a specific type of building, for example, the picture of the castle on page 2 of *The playroom*. Then, using postcards, cut-outs from magazines, photocopies and tracings from books and worksheets, build up a collection of pictures of household items that would have been found in that type of building. When a particular period of the past is being studied, or if one of the class wants to write a story set in a certain time, then this visual dictionary can be used as a useful resource for background scenery and details.

Art

The children could make a picture of a building while it is being built. Encourage them to include as much information as possible by adding suitable labels for windows, ceilings, doorways, etc. They might be able to add a few technical terms, such as lintels, foundations, joists, jambs.

Geography

Ask the children to make a map of Jake's journey in *The chimney sweep*. Make sure their plans show the progress of the characters from Mr Webster's house to the Manor House, and include Jake's journey up the chimney, across the roof and into the bedrooms. To brighten up the map the children may like to add pictures of the characters involved in the story at key points on the journey.

Design Technology

You could help children make 3D models of different buildings. They could make a thatched roof for a medieval cottage by using straw, straws or corrugated cardboard. Wattle walls can be made by weaving strips of card together. They can then be smothered in daub made from a gooey mixture of glue, sawdust, ground up chalk, dry powder paint, and sand.

The children could make stones for later houses by casting them out of plaster. Mix the plaster to a thick consistency and pour it into matchbox trays or an old ice cube tray. This will give you building blocks of a regular size.

For further ideas on making models you may find it useful to look at *Build your own model house* (Fact Finders Unit C), *Build a model of your school* (More Unit C; to be published Spring 1997).

IT

The children could build up a simple database that contains details of the different buildings that appear in the *Jackdaws* and *More Jackdaws*. You could have fields for roof shapes, room sizes, number of storeys and different materials.

RE

You could arrange visits to religious buildings, such as synagogues, mosques, temples, churches, chapels. Tell the children about famous religious buildings, for example: the mosque of the Dome of the Rock in Jerusalem; the mosque at Mecca; the Golden Temple at Amritsar; St Paul's Cathedral.

Book list

Story books

From the *Oxford Reading Tree*
The broken roof (Owls, Stage 7) ; *The photograph* (Robins, Stage 9); *The holiday* (Robins, Stage 10)

Other story books

Allen Ahlberg *Miss Brick the Builder's Baby* (Picture Puffin)
Lucy Boston *The children of Green Knowe, The chimneys of Green Knowe* (Penguin)
Gillian Cross *Save our school* (Methuen)
Clive King *Stig of the dump* (Puffin)
Graham Oakley *The church mice stories* (Picturemac)
All round the city (Reading 360 Level 6, Ginn)

Poetry books

From the *Oxford Reading Tree*
Castle Poems (*More Jackdaws* poetry)

Other poetry books

Marian Lines 'Building site' from *A first poetry book* edited by John Foster (Oxford University Press)
M Livingstone *Buildings* (Young Puffin)
G Owen 'The building site' from *Song of the city* (Young Lions)
Jack Prelutsky 'Haunted house' from *A very first poetry book* edited by John Foster (Oxford University Press)
J Tippet 'Building a skyscraper' *Once upon a rhyme* (Young Puffin)

Information books

David J Brown *How they were built* (Kingfisher Books)
R Daizell *We can build it* (Cherrytree books)
Andrew Haslam *Make it Work: Building* (Two Can)
Fiona Macdonald and John James *Inside Story: A Medieval Castle* (Simon & Schuster)
Fiona Macdonald *Timelines: Houses* (Watling)
G Rickard *Bricks* (Wayland)
P Steele *I wonder why...Castles had moats* (Kingfisher)
Philip Wilkinson *Eyewitness: Building* (Dorling Kindersley)
Incredible Castles and Knights (Snapshot)

Transport

The following *Oxford Reading Tree* books could be read as part of this topic:

The spoilt holiday, Danger at sea, and *In the snow* (Jackdaws); *Space adventure, The playroom, The snow storm, The secret cave, The island,* and *The chimney sweep* (More Jackdaws)

Discussion

Types of transport: There are many different types of transport mentioned in the *Jackdaws* and *More Jackdaws*.

Can the children think of them all? Which types of transport have they used? Which would they most like to use?

Journeys: Encourage the children to talk about different journeys they have made. Which was the most exciting? Why? Which was the most uncomfortable? Why?

Difficult choices: You could either talk about a real example or an imaginary place. Because so many more people are driving in Town X there has to be a new car park. There is no spare land for this so it will have to be built in a place where there are already buildings or public spaces. These places might include a park, a children's play area, some allotments, a residential area, a shopping street, an area of old people's housing, a pub, a place of historical interest, a church. Whatever is already on the land will have to be pulled down. Encourage different children to talk about the places they would choose for the car park. Finish the discussion by asking the children to vote for the place they think would be most suitable for the car park – or would they vote against building the car park at all?

Art

Ask the children to think of their three favourite forms of transport. Tell them to find illustrations of these types of transport or to cut pictures from magazines. Tell them to combine these types of transport into one. They could do this by drawing a large picture or making a collage. What will they call their new invention? What could it be used for? Would it be fast or slow?

Maths

The children could construct simple bar graphs to compare the speeds of different types of transport. The bar chart could be based on a hypothetical set of results, such as those given below; or the data could be obtained from observation and measurement.

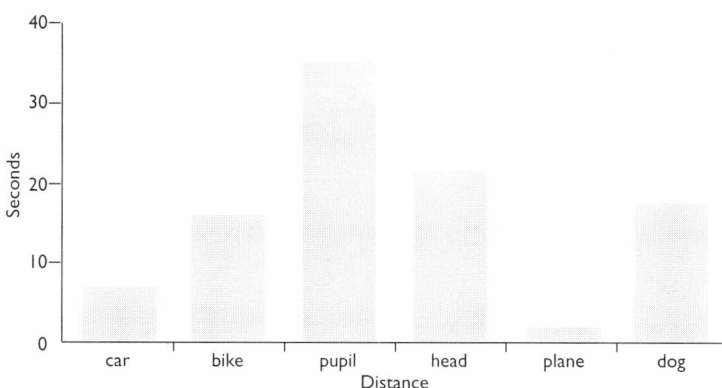

This is how long it takes different kinds of transport to cover 100 metres: a car takes 7 seconds; a mountain bike takes 16 seconds; a pupil in Year 2 takes 34 seconds; a head teacher takes 22 seconds; a plane takes 1 second; a dog takes 17 seconds.

Presenting mathematical information in the form of a bar chart makes problem-solving relatively easy. It is a particularly good method of making comparisons and coming to conclusions about sets of results.

Science

The children could make a fleet of boats from identical yoghurt pots. Ask them to predict how they think the pots will perform as boats. Will they stay upright? Will they fill with water? Give each child a lump of plasticine. Ask them to find out how much plasticine they need and where to put it so that the yoghurt pots will float upright.

When all the yoghurt pots are floating in an upright position ask the children to think of ways they can propel the pots without touching them. The most obvious force to use is blowing. An alternative is to agitate the water behind the pots so that the force of the waves moves the pots. Which force is the most effective? Is it possible to control the direction in which the yoghurt pots move?

Ask the children to try and embed a lolly stick or straw in the plasticine. Before they put the boats back in the water ask the children to predict whether these masts will make the boats more or less stable. When the boats are floating ask the children to investigate the effects of blowing on the masts.

Wait and see if any of the class suggest adding sails. What do they find is the most effective sail shape?

Design Technology

Collect cardboard rolls, cotton reels, thin card from cereal packets, straws, string, paper and margarine tubs and their lids of various shapes and sizes. Spread these materials out on a table top. Tell the children to look at the pictures on pages 22, 26, 27 and 29 of *Danger at sea*. Point out that the picture on page 27 shows that the wrecked ship was a paddle steamer. Encourage the children to compare the shapes of the different craft with the shapes of the materials in front of them.

The children could draw a simple sketch plan to show how they could use the different materials to make a model of one of the craft featured in the book. When the children have made their models a diorama (a three-dimensional scene) could be constructed to display some of the different models. Real stones could be used to represent the rocks; painted, crumpled paper could be used for the waves. Do not worry if the size of the margarine tubs means that the rowing boat and the paddle steamer are almost the same size. Placing the bigger boat at the back of the diorama will give a feeling of perspective.

Geography

A display of pictures of different types of transport cut from magazines, traced or copied from books could be assembled around a map of the world. This will help the children make comparisons about the transport used in different parts of the world. They could see, for example, how the Chinese tend to use bicycles rather than cars. Charities such as Save the Children and Oxfam can supply information on transport systems in some poorer countries of the world. Make sure the children realize that people in these countries also use cars, trains, buses, planes.

History

Help the children to use the non-fiction resources of the school or local library to research the dates of key moments in the history of transport. Alternatively, tell them stories of the key events. Ask them to draw pictures of such events as the Viking explorations of England and America, Sir Francis Drake's circumnavigation of the world, the opening of the Stockton to Darlington railway, the Montgolfier brothers' balloon ascent, Henry Ford's mass production of the Model T, the Wright Brothers' first powered flight, the opening of the M1, the first moon landing. Arrange all these events in a time-line.

Drama

The children could mime going on journeys in different types of transport. Can the other children guess what kind of transport they are using?

RE

You could talk to the children about pilgrimage to holy places. Explain that this idea is common to all the main world religions and how for the people of some faiths it is very important to visit the holy places at least once in a lifetime, for example, Muslims to Mecca, Bahais to Israel. Other examples of religious pilgrimages are Hindus going to bathe in the River Ganges; Sikhs going to the Golden Temple at Amritsar; Jews going to the Wailing Wall in Jerusalem; Christians going to Lourdes, Jerusalem, Canterbury.

Book list

Story books
From the *Oxford Reading Tree*
The flying carpet (*Magpies* Stage 8)

Other story books
Hans Christian Andersen *The Snow Queen* (Picture Puffin)
Edward Ardizzone *Ship's Cook Ginger* (Bodley Head)
Edward Ardizzone *Tim to the rescue* (Picture Puffin)
Quentin Blake *Mrs Armitage on wheels* (Picture Lions)
Geraldine McCaughrean *The Canterbury Tales* (Oxford University Press)
Geraldine McCaughrean *The Odyssey* (Oxford University Press)
Judy Gilbert and Adele Graham *The Bugs' Bus* (Sunshine Books Heinemann Education)
Graham Greene and Edward Ardizzone *The Little Fire Engine. The Little Train, The Little Horse Bus, The Little Steamroller* (Viking)
Colin and Jacqui Hawkins *Come for a Ride on The Ghost Train* (Walker)
Norman Hunter *Professor Branestawm's Pocket Motor Car* (Puffin)
Rodney Peppe *The Mice and the Travel Machine, The Mice and the Clockwork Bus* (Viking)
John Ryan *Pugwash and the ghost ship* (Picture Puffin)
Angie Sage *The Little Blue Book of the Marie Celeste* (Puffin)
Dora Thatcher *Lizzie the lifeboat* (Hodder and Stoughton)
Martin Waddell and Philippe Dupasquier *Going West* (Puffin)
J Webster *Karen's bike* (Ginn)
J Willis *Dr Xargle's book of earth mobiles* (Puffin)

Poetry books
From the *Oxford Reading Tree*
Transport poems, Home Poems (*Conkers*); *Space Poems, Star Poems* (*More Jackdaws* poetry)

Other poetry books
Jill Bennet *Machine Poems* (Oxford University Press)
Russell Hoban 'Esme on her brother's bicycle' in *Moving along* (Evans)
Brian Moses 'Rocket horse' from *Another first poetry book* (Oxford University Press)
Brian Patten *The Magic Bicycle* (Walker)
Full fathom five, Shakespeare poems for under 7 year-olds (Kestrel)

Information books

Eileen Browne and David Parkins *No Problem* (Activity book, Walker Books)

N Davies *Oceans* (BBC)

Ian Graham *How it Goes: Boats* (Watts Books)

B James *Polar regions* (Wayland)

Frank McCormick *Experiments with Flight* (Cherrytree Books)

Andrew Nahum *Panorama: A History of Road Transport – From Chariots to Cadillacs*

Chris Oxlade *The X-Ray Picture book of Fantastic Transport Machines* (Walker Books)

A Rockwell *Trucks* (Picture Puffin)

A Rockwell *Bikes* (Picture Puffin)

Katrina Siliprandi *Victorian Transport* (Wayland)

T Wood *Lifeboat* (Franklin Watts)

Eyewitness: Boat (Dorling Kindersley)

Ships and sailing (Dorling Kindersley)

Plays

From the *Oxford Reading Tree*

Rod Hunt, Jacquie Buttriss, Ann Callendar *The flying carpet* (*Magpie* Stage 8 playscript)

Oxford Reading Tree: Jackdaws anthologies

Name . . . . Date started . . . .

Date completed . . . .

Jackdaws and More Jackdaws	Date	Comments
Jackdaws		
The spoilt holiday		
Anna's eggs		
Patrick and the fox		
Danger at sea		
Karen's adventure		
Kate's garden		
In the snow		
The catch		
William and the ghost		
William and the mouse		
More Jackdaws		
The school play		
The jokers		
William and the spell		
Space adventure		
Monkey business		
The playroom		
The snow storm		
The secret cave		
The island		
The chimney sweep		

**Oxford
Reading
Tree**

Name . . . .

Date . . . .

Running record sheet
from *Jackdaws* **Stage 8** ***Anna's eggs* pages 12–13**

Introduction

Talk about the story so far. Where did Auntie Jo have to go? What had Auntie Jo asked Anna to do?

Anna ran out to the door of the shed and shouted, 'Help! Mum! Come and see what I've done!'

'What's the matter?' asked Mum as she came into the shed. 'Let me have a look.'

Anna showed her the cracked eggs. 'I didn't do anything,' she said, 'but the eggs are all broken!'

Before she could say another word, one of the eggs gave a little wobble. A small hole appeared in the shell. Out of the hole poked a tiny yellow beak. Suddenly the shell split open and a little, wet chicken struggled out.

'It's a chicken!' shouted Anna.

99 words

1 Where were the eggs?
2 What makes you think Anna is upset?
3 What did Anna think she had done?
4 What was happening to the eggs?
5 Can you think of another word for 'split'?

Retelling

Types of miscues/reading strategies . . . .

Number of words read accurately

Percentage accuracy

**Oxford
Reading
Tree**

Name . . . .

Date . . . .

Running record sheet

from *More Jackdaws* Stage 9 *William and the spell* pages 8–9

Introduction

Talk about the story so far. Why had William gone to the library? What did William's mum think William spent too much time doing?

The children's storybooks were in a special room in one corner of the library. To get into it William had to go through a door which was so small that only children could use it. On the door was a notice which said 'NO GROWN-UPS'. On the walls were pictures of characters from storybooks, and around the room were comfortable chairs where the children could sit and read. 'This is good,' thought William, 'but it's a shame there's no television. I wish my bedroom had a special small door. Then Mum would never know it was untidy.' There were so many books William wanted to read that it was very difficult to make a choice.

115 words

1 Why did the room have a small door?
2 What did the room have in it that made children want to sit and read?
3 Why did William wish his room at home could have a small door?
4 Why did William find it difficult to choose a book?
5 What did William think was missing from the room?

Retelling

Types of miscues/reading strategies . . . .

Number of words read accurately

Percentage accuracy

Oxford Reading Tree

Name . . . .

Date . . . .

Running record sheet

from *Jackdaws* Stage 10 *Karen's adventure* page 17

Introduction

Talk about the story so far. Where was Karen staying? What was in the box Karen found in the old greenhouse? What warning was written on the lid of the box? What happened to the egg? Where did Karen hide the dragon?

It rained all afternoon. Gran wouldn't let Karen go outside. 'You can't go out in this, dear, you'll get soaked,' she said.

'I'll just have to give the dragon two breakfasts tomorrow,' thought Karen. That night there was another storm. The dragon came out of the greenhouse and climbed over the wall. He made his way towards the house and climbed through the kitchen window. He was looking for something to eat.

In the fridge was a roast chicken. The dragon opened the fridge door and took the chicken in his jaws. With a single gulp he swallowed it whole.

100 words

1 Why did Karen want to go out?
2 Why did the dragon come into the house?
3 What is important about the roast chicken?
4 What does 'he swallowed it whole' mean?

Retelling

Types of miscues/reading strategies . . . .

Number of words read accurately

Percentage accuracy

**Oxford
Reading
Tree**

Name . . . .

Date . . . .

Running record sheet
from *More Jackdaws* Stage 11   *The island* page 12

Introduction

Talk about the story so far. Why did Mr Campbell want to buy the island? What was Mr Campbell planning to do with the ruined castle? What was the strange legend connected with the castle?

'A very fine story, Mrs McKay, and one that is going to make me a great deal of money.' Nobody had noticed Mr Campbell standing in the doorway of the workshop.

'I've come to make you one last offer, Mrs McKay,' said Campbell. 'Next week I start building. Without your land it's going to be very difficult to bring ashore the men and machinery I need to start work on the castle. But if you won't sell, you can be sure I'll find another way.'

He took a cheque out of his pocket. 'Here's a cheque for fifty thousand pounds. It's my final offer.'

102 words

1 What job did Mrs McKay do?
2 Where did Mrs McKay live?
3 What was Mr Campbell going to bring to the island?
4 What is a 'cheque'?

Retelling

Types of miscues/reading strategies . . . .

Number of words read accurately

Percentage accuracy

Book review

Name _____

I have chosen _____

by _____

The main characters are _____

_____

_____

I liked the part when _____

_____

_____

_____

_____

I think you will like this book because _____

_____

_____